Yourself.
Your Marriage.
Your Children.
Your Business.
Your Money.
Your World
and Your God.

**Is there anything
more important
to think about?**

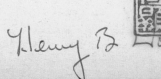

FOR MEN ONLY

The Dynamics of Being a Man and Succeeding at It

Edited by
J. ALLAN PETERSEN

LIVING BOOKS
Tyndale House Publishers, Inc.
Wheaton, Illinois

TO THE FOUR MEN IN MY LIFE

— my father, John P. Petersen

— my sons, John, Ray, and Paul

First printing, Living Books Edition, March 1982

Library of Congress Catalog Card Number 72-97655, paper
81-84764, Living Books Edition
ISBN: 8423-0891-1, paper
8423-0892-X, Living Books Edition

Copyright © 1973 by Tyndale House Publishers,
Wheaton, Illinois 60187.

Printed in the United States of America

Contents

Acknowledgments

"First, Love Yourself!" by Harold R. Nelson, is condensed and reprinted by permission from the December 30, 1966, *Covenant Companion,* 5101 N. Francisco, Chicago, Ill.

"Remove That Wall," by William E. Hulme, is reprinted by permission from *Living with Myself,* copyright © 1964 Prentice-Hall, Inc., Englewood Cliffs, N.J.

"Impossibility Thinking," by Robert H. Schuller, is condensed from *Move Ahead with Possibility Thinking,* copyright © 1967 by the author. Used by permission of Doubleday & Co., Inc., Garden City, N.Y.

"How to Motivate," by W. Clement Stone, is reprinted by permission from *Nation's Business,* copyright © 1968 Chamber of Commerce of the U.S., Washington, D.C.

"Mark It Maturity," by Richard Shelley Taylor, is reprinted by permission from *The Disciplined Life,* copyright © 1962 Beacon Hill Press, Kansas City, Mo.

"Man, the Leader," by David Augsburger, is reprinted by permission from *Cherishable: Love and Marriage,* copyright © 1971 Herald Press, Scottdale, Pa.

"This Is Love," by Theodor Bovet, is abridged from *Love, Skill, and Marriage,* copyright © 1950 Longmans, Green & Co., Ltd. Used by permission of Doubleday & Co., Inc., Garden City, N.Y.

"Your Wife's Psychologist," by Paul Plattner, is adapted from *Conflict and Understanding in Marriage,* copyright © 1970 M. E. Bratcher. Used by permission of John Knox Press, Richmond, Va.

"Rx for Marital Illness," by A. Dudley Dennison, M.D., is condensed from *Give It to Me Straight, Doctor,* copyright © 1972 Zondervan Publishing House, Grand Rapids, Mich. Used by permission.

"Make Her Happy," by Cecil G. Osborne, is condensed from *The Art of Understanding Your Mate,* copyright © 1970 Zondervan Publishing House, Grand Rapids, Mich. Used by permission.

"When the Wine Runs Out," by G. R. Slater, is reprinted by permission from *Marriage Is for Living,* copyright © 1968 Zondervan Publishing House, Grand Rapids, Mich.

"Like Father, Like Son," by Leslie Flynn, is condensed from Chapter 8 of *Your Influence Is Showing,* copyright © 1967 Broadman Press, Nashville, Tenn. Used by permission.

"Fathers of Orphans," by Joel Nederhood, is condensed from *Radio Pulpit.* Used by permission of The Back to God Hour of the Christian Reformed Church, 10858 S. Michigan, Chicago, Ill.

"Help Your Son Become a Man," by Anetta Bridges, is condensed from the January 1972 issue of *Success Unlimited,* Chicago, Ill. Used by permission.

"Dad, Your Daughter Needs You," by John E. Crawford, is condensed from *Being the Real Father Now That Your Teen-Ager Will*

Preface

There are many books on the market for women: how to be a fascinating woman, a contented wife, a capable mother. Women are analyzed, evaluated, and instructed on everything from their spiritual qualities to their sex appeal.

But why is not more written for men? From the superabundance of books for and about women and the scarcity of books for men, you could conclude that women need the most help.

I don't buy that. The Bible and human history teach us that a man is made for leadership in the society and the home. And when strong, confident, masculine leadership is lacking, a vacuum is created which is invaded by demonic and destructive forces.

As God observed the moral deterioration and social decadence of Israel, he said, "Where are the men? . . . I sought for a man among them that should make up the hedge, and stand in the gap before me for the land that I should not destroy it, but I found none" (Ezekiel 22:30). God depends on the presence of committed and responsible men to maintain a righteous society and to represent him on the earth.

This book brings into focus the areas of a man's world where actions make the difference between existence and life, struggle and fulfillment. The array of wise, experienced authors give counsel in religious and secular fields, dealing with the inner life and outer actions. Like a seven-course meal, its chapters will be enjoyed separately as well as all at one sitting. There is continuity, yet great variety.

On my visits to the post office, I see notices of "WANTED" men. Despite the publicity and supersleuthing, many are never found. This book is a part of God's program to find and build men who can lead families and communities, men who will live now to change eternity.

J. Allan Petersen
Omaha, Nebraska

1

The Man and Himself

FIRST, LOVE YOURSELF!

by Harold R. Nelson

*Director, Department of Pastoral Care,
Swedish Covenant Hospital, Chicago*

"Do you love yourself?"

On several occasions when I have asked groups this question, I have received a puzzled and embarrassed reaction. Only a very few felt able to raise their hands unashamedly and affirmatively.

However, the Bible encourages the love of self. When Jesus was asked by a Pharisee to name the greatest commandment, he immediately tied together the two basic Old Testament laws of love. The first was that you should love God with your total being, the second that you "love your neighbor as yourself."

Why do people avoid, or appear to avoid, loving themselves?

My first hunch is that many people identify love of self with selfishness. They don't want to say good about themselves for fear of being accused of conceit and vanity. However, having a positive self-regard is quite different from conceit.

To call attention to yourself repeatedly in monopolizing conversation or some strange form of behavior is to reveal you really do not love yourself. The conceited person's problem is precisely that he loves himself too little, not too much.

Another hunch I have about why people don't want to love themselves is that it clashes with the Christian concept of self-denial. Some feel that we can't both love and deny ourselves.

Because of deep and chronic inferiority feelings, some Christians have identified the gospel with self-degradation and contempt. The lower they can get, the more Christian they feel. But we can deny ourselves only as we learn to love ourselves, for false humility is a cover-up for a "bad me" image. Those who wear a mask of false humility are just as starved for love as those who wear the mask of conceit.

People also evade loving themselves to avoid responsibility. If you say, as many do, that you are not "good enough," you won't have to take a responsibility offered you.

This is precisely what the slothful servant did in the parable of the talents (Matthew 25:25). Being afraid that he had nothing to give, he hid his talent in the ground. Specifically, if he had been able to love himself, he could have made a profit for his master. All of us waste opportunities to be of help to a fellow human being because we did not believe ourselves "adequate" or "good enough." We did not want to take the risk of failure but rather remained sealed in the womb of inferiority — comfortable in our little world and not daring to reach out into the human mess around us.

The opposite of love of self is hatred of self, and a struggle between the two will always go on within us.

Patterns of self-hate begin in infancy and perhaps even in the prenatal stage. The baby who is not wanted is bound to feel that rejection. Emotionally defenseless, he will pick up the rejection and form a "bad me" self-image. Later, protective defenses will be formed to insulate against further hurt. Unfortunately, some children may be hurt so badly that they will never want to risk a close loving relationship, but by and large, most of our children have had enough love along with the hurt to be able to give and receive some love.

Self-hatred is expressed today in many ways. One of the most concrete is suicide. Each year in the U. S. some 18,000 persons feel so completely worthless that they destroy themselves. A much more subtle form of self-hatred can be seen in alcoholism. Feeling little self-esteem, the alcoholic turns to the bottle, where for awhile he becomes "king of the mountain." An estimated eight million Americans are committing slow suicide through this means. The number-one health problem of our day — mental illness — afflicts a host of people unable to stand themselves as they are, all seeking love but not knowing how to find it or to receive it if they find it.

All of us have our own ways of hating or degrading ourselves. You may do it by being a hard-working perfectionist, and I may do it by being a disorganized, lazy nonconformist. If all you know is "work and achieve," you may be consciously or unconsciously trying to prove your worth to yourself and others.

Among other ways we depreciate ourselves is to indulge in rampant inferiority feelings. Perhaps this is one reason the Christian Church has failed to get deeply involved in the needs of society. Rather than using the gospel as a source of power to love self and neighbor, some have misused it to impose more guilt and self-punishment.

What has to take place for me to become loving toward myself? First of all, one does not learn to love himself in isolation. We learn to love ourselves as we enter into personal relationship with both God and man, and the relationship we have with God is very closely tied to the one we have with man. When we receive love from God we open up a line to receive from our brother, and when we receive love from our brother we also receive it from God (1 John 4:20).

Three important encounters must be experienced in order for me to love myself. The first is *self-awareness*. If I am to love myself, I must know what I am and am not. I must be able to look critically at myself and be aware of both my weaknesses and strengths.

This is not easy. To let defenses come down and admit a weakness can be a fearful and confusing experience. For example, if I need to maintain an image of myself as a nice, even-tempered guy, chances are that underneath I have an explosive temper. Repression is the capacity to put out of my sight that which I do not want to see in myself. However, that does not mean that in wanting to appear even-tempered I have gotten rid of my temper. Under pressure it will erupt like a forgotten volcano. Why resist self-awareness? If God already knows me as I am, it is ridiculous for me to put on a mask before him.

A second encounter is *self-acceptance*. Here I gain the freedom to be what I am. I can say, "This is me — this is where I stand right now." I am able to accept myself because God in Christ has accepted me as I am. He did not say, "I will accept you if . . ." but, "I will accept you in spite of your shortcomings and failures." If God in Christ has truly accepted me as I am, should I do less? Ironically, many Christians refuse to accept themselves even when God has fully accepted them.

Self-acceptance is closely tied with the capacity to receive forgiveness of my sins. The one who cannot forgive self is the one who cannot accept self. When we accept ourselves as we are, then we become free to change. All the efforts we put into self-reform — New Year's resolutions included — are in vain if underneath is still an unacceptable self. The wife who strives to reform an alcoholic husband usually drives him into more drinking. When the wife can let her alcoholic husband be what he is, then he can begin to admit his need and hopefully to move toward a helping hand.

To accept yourself you must start where you are. Our love for ourselves can be great enough to accept whatever we are when we know God's love for us is greater still.

The third encounter that needs to happen, and keep happening, is *self-giving*. You are to love yourself in order to give love to others. The narcissist attempts to turn all love toward himself and is threatened at the thought of giving something of himself to another. This is a self-defeating game, for no one can endure a lasting relationship with a person who takes all but gives nothing in return. Give love to others, and you will get it back.

You are to "love your neighbor as yourself." This means the self-acceptance you feel should spontaneously be communicated to your neighbor — spontaneously because this is something you should not have to stop and think about. Loving self and neighbor is never easy or complete, but it is the repeated starting point for authentic journeys to life's goals.

THE WORLD NEEDS MEN

. . . *who cannot be bought;*
. . . *whose word is their bond;*
. . . *who put character above wealth;*
. . . *who possess opinions and a will;*
. . . *who are larger than their vocations;*
. . . *who do not hesitate to take chances.*
. . . *who will not lose their individuality in a crowd;*
. . . *who will be as honest in small things as in great things;*
. . . *who will make no compromise with wrong.*
. . . *whose ambitions are not confined to their own selfish desires;*
. . . *who will not say they do it "because everybody else does it."*
. . . *who are true to their friends through good report and evil report, in adversity as well as in prosperity.*
. . . *who do not believe that shrewdness, cunning, and hardheadedness are the best qualities for winning success;*
. . . *who are not ashamed or afraid to stand for the truth when it is unpopular, who can say "no" with emphasis, although all the rest of the world says "yes."*

REMOVE THAT WALL

by William Hulme

Professor of Pastoral Care,
Luther Seminary, St. Paul, Minnesota

The students at the seminary where I teach have a year of internship before their last year of study. Some serve as student chaplains in institutions where they work with physicians and psychiatrists. I was visiting with a couple who were friends of a student who had recently completed his internship, and the conversation took the following turn: "I don't know — I just don't like to be around Jack as much as I used to," the woman said.

"How come?" I asked.

"Well," she continued, "with all that psychology he had last year I have the feeling he is analyzing everything I say — looking right through me."

"You don't like that?" I asked.

"No," she answered, "I don't."

I was probably feeling sadistic that night for I needled: "Something you want to hide?"

Her husband chivalrously came to her defense. "After all," he said, "who doesn't have something he wants to hide!"

I think we all know what he meant. When we mentally isolate ourselves from others — living at some point with ourselves alone — we are living with something to hide.

I remember that as a child I hid behind the door when the music teacher arrived to give me my first piano lesson. Although I knew that this was no permanent solution to my problem, I was at least postponing the moment of reckoning.

The tendency to hide has been our first line of defense since Adam tried to avoid God in the Garden of Eden. Regardless of how temporary the security is, we are comforted by the fact that we are unexposed at least for now. Actually, we are indulging in a childish game of hide and seek: we are secure only if we stay out of sight; but if we stay hidden we will not be able to reach the goal. Fear gives excessive priority to the present tense.

Basically, we use three ways to try to protect ourselves from exposure: withdrawal from others; servile attachment to others; and attack on others. Each of these ways offers temporary security for a stiff price — a person forfeits the possibility of genuine relationship with others. Although each way differs radically from the others in approach, they all express profound distrust of human nature. They are based upon the axiom: others will hurt me if they can, therefore I must not allow myself to become vulnerable.

The *way of withdrawal* consists in putting a safe distance between ourselves and others. The strategy is that you cannot see me if I do not get close to you, and if you cannot see me you cannot hurt me.

The person who withdraws is often shy — he fears being rejected by others. He can erect a wall around his inner self so that people think they know him when they do not. This psychological wall permits him to see into others but prevents them from seeing into him. Thus he can safely make contact with others without becoming involved with them. There is no sharing and no participation, only observation.

Few of us consciously withdraw as a protection from people. Instead of tracing our withdrawal to fear, we regard it as indifference. "I don't want to" sounds better to everyone than "I'm afraid to."

In group sessions where individuals are sharing with each other, one or two may remain aloof. Although they may comment or give advice to those who do share, they never share anything of themselves. When pressed by the group to truly participate, they usually declare they have no need to share. At best this creates the impression that they are fully self-sufficient, at worst that they are smugly looking down on the others.

A maturing adult may detach himself emotionally from others to compensate for his lack of acceptance. He resists involvement for fear of exposing himself to further hurt.

He walls up his shaky confidence with an air of aloofness, hiding his true need for others behind a façade of self-sufficiency.

The *way of servile attachment* is based on the idea that others will be tolerant of my foibles if I make myself congenial and indispensable. Here the individual concentrates on making friendly and helpful overtures to others instead of ignoring them. But behind the kindly façade is a frightened individual who has serious misgivings about his own worth. His apparent congeniality and generosity have their price: a superficial loyalty and a smothered individuality.

A person who effaces himself in order to please others is known as a "nice guy." He is also regarded as a "lightweight" in accomplishment. Because he offers no threat, there is no reason to attack him, but there is also no reason to rate him as important for he is easily taken for granted and his sensitivities can be ignored. Yet even the servile person has individuality. He may hide his individuality behind a disarming smile which he wears even when relating bad news. In counseling with such an individual, the counselor knows that so long as the conversation is accompanied by the smile the real person is not coming through. But there are those moments when the real person does break through — when the hidden facts unexpectedly emerge into the open. These are heavy, even depressing moments, but they are honest moments. It is then that the smile departs, for it is no longer needed.

Have you noticed how much more polite people are when they are walking than when they are driving an automobile? The automobile seems to provide all the protection needed from people and so they can more safely expose their aggressive tendencies. Similarly, people will speak more boldly to each other in a group than when only two acquaintances face each other. Two self-protective people have a fear of rupturing the rapport, and they avoid overtures that would create conflict. Thus their friendliness stops short of assisting another to face an unpleasant truth. It is much easier for them to apologize than to criticize.

Emotionally, they are more predisposed to guilt than to anger.

The *way of attack* is preventive warfare. The idea is to go after others before they come after you. The aggressive nature of this protective device seems to belie the fact that it is motivated by fear. Even people who are servilely congenial may attack when their hidden hostility becomes too much to hold back or their strategy of servility encounters humiliating failure.

People who choose the way of attack believe that the best defense is a good offense. For them life is a meanly competitive business. The only way to keep others from putting you in the doghouse is to put them in first, for if you give people the opportunity they will take advantage of you. Beneath this uncomplimentary image of others lies the hidden uncomplimentary image of the self. If I am this way, then they must be this way also. And if they are — I am in danger. Therefore the only way to survive in such an arena is by using openly competitive tactics.

This is basically the point of view of the wrestler. His survival depends upon being on top of someone else. Alarm occurs when the other person gets on top, producing an imminent threat of defeat. Security depends on not being put into such a vulnerable position.

The attack may be direct as well as indirect. We can pick on people and exasperate them. We can do this openly by simply bullying people, or (and this is more often the case) we can subtly make them feel stupid and inadequate. There are many "innocent" ways in which this can be done.

The more we know a person the more we know where his sensitivities lie. This is why brothers and sisters can torment each other so effectively and why husbands and wives undermine each other's confidence so efficiently. Each has discovered through the privileges of intimacy the whereabouts of his partner's Achilles' heel. Each knows how to hit the glass jaw and to pummel the solar plexus. In moments of hostility each abuses his privilege and takes advantage of his knowledge.

In contrast to the person who is servile, the attacker is a poor apologizer with proneness to hostility rather than guilt. Those who attack give no quarter and usually ask for none. Consequently, they are the most difficult group to help.

If you recognized your own actions in any of the devices described above, I am sure the discovery made you unhappy. Though these devices are designed to protect us, they add to our damaged self-image. When we withdraw, we heighten our awareness that we have something to hide. When we behave slavishly, we are aware that much of this behavior is a façade. When we attack, we are aware that we are in-flicting hurt.

Any contrast between our inner self and our outer self registers negatively on our conscience — even as it blocks our relationship with others. Although we may be con-sciously unaware of our self-centered motivations, they nonetheless take their toll of our self-respect.

We can recognize ourselves in the mirror if we stand directly in front of it, but we resist the direct gaze. When we receive an assist from without, however, we may be able really to see ourselves. The result is always upsetting, yet it can be the beginning of a more honest relationship with ourselves.

Life is a lively process of becoming. If you haven't added to your interest during the past year; if you are thinking the same thoughts, relating the same personal experiences, having the same predic-table reactions — rigor mortis of the personality has set in.

—GENERAL DOUGLAS MACARTHUR

IMPOSSIBILITY THINKING

by Robert H. Schuller

Pastor, Garden Grove
Community Church, California

There are two kinds of people in the world: possibility thinkers and impossibility thinkers. Which are you?

To find out, take this test. Answer honestly as you ask yourself these questions:

1. Do I look for reasons why something can't be done instead of searching for ways in which it can be done?

2. Do I ever make decisions out of fear?

3. Do I tend to resist new ideas and prefer to do things the way I've always done them?

4. Do I move ahead only when I have every single fact?

5. Do I have a tendency to demand a guarantee of success before I begin?

6. Do I imagine the opposition I will encounter without imagining the support I might expect?

7. Do I ever turn down an idea simply because I don't like it or because my mind is already made up or because I've made other plans?

8. Do I ever close my mind to a suggestion before hearing the full explanation?

9. Do I point out the disadvantages in an idea before I point out the advantages?

10. Do I ever make negative decisions because I am tired and it's easier?

11. If I can't imagine a solution to a problem, am I inclined to turn away from it?

12. Do I believe that human nature can't really be altered; that a man's life can't be changed?

If you have answered many of these questions in the affirmative, then the chances are very good that you are suffering from an impossibility complex.

However, you can overcome that impossibility complex.

You can become a possibility thinker if you want to become one.

Great discipline generates enormous strength. The Russian psychologist Pavlov "invented" a procedure which is at the basis of what is popularly called "brainwashing." It has been used negatively by Communists. But it can be used as a positive, constructive, healing, life-transforming procedure. Constantly feeding the brain positive thoughts will eventually transform the thinking procedure.

Now try this eight-step treatment for the impossibility complex. If you believe these eight points, if you really follow each point religiously, your life will change. The world around you will change. For you will have changed your thinking. Transformed thinking transforms everything.

1. Remove your disadvantage complex. Don't be tricked, tripped, and trapped by these disadvantage complexes if one or more are bothering you.

"I'm too old."

You are not too old to change until you give up. You are not old until you have lost your vision. That's why thousands of octogenarians have astonished the world with the sudden discovery of talents that lay buried deep within them for over eighty years before they were discovered. Grandma Moses is only one example.

"I'm handicapped."

The most serious handicap any person can have is an impossibility complex (and you are breaking that right now). My wife has a cousin named Frank Vander Maaten. At the age of eighteen he was one of the most accomplished violinists in Sioux County, Iowa. Then a terrible accident happened in his father's blacksmith shop. A red-hot iron fell on his left hand. The four fingers that touched the strings of his violin were cut off! Only his thumb remained on his mutilated hand. Handicapped? Not in his thinking! He determined to learn to play the violin left-handed. And he did, holding the bow in his mutilated hand. He became a prominent violinist in the Sioux City Symphony. You are not handicapped until you think you are.

"I am from a lowly background."

So what? No one's background or past is a disadvantage unless he makes it so in his thinking! Remember, any disadvantage rightly handled can be turned into an advantage. A young man with a "hillbilly" background could have allowed himself to develop an inferiority complex when he came to the big city. But he was honest, friendly, natural, warm, and instead of letting his "disadvantage" work against him, he turned it to his advantage. I am referring to Tennessee Ernie Ford.

"My skin is not the right color."

You can do, or be, almost anything you can dream or desire. Robert Weaver, the first American Negro to hold cabinet office, had this idea drummed into him as a child by his mother: "The way to offset color prejudice is to be awfully good at whatever you do."

"My I.Q. is lower than others'."

So what? First prizes don't always go to the brightest and strongest man. Again and again, the man who wins is the man who is sure that he can.

2. *Develop the habit of recognizing and responding to the smallest trickle of positivism that might leak into your mind.* One small possibility thought can overpower many impossibility thoughts, if the possibility thought is given a chance to survive and thrive.

3. *Begin each day with a positive seed thought and hold it there.* Make a hobby of collecting "shields for the spirit" that can fortify your mind as you move into the workaday world. Try these spirit shields:

Luke 1:37 — "With God nothing shall be impossible."

Mark 10:27 — "With men it is impossible, but not with God."

Matthew 19:26 — "But with God all things are possible."

Mark 9:23 — "If you can believe, all things are possible to him who believes."

Our family eats breakfast together. Before we scatter our separate ways, we have our "spiritual vitamin" for the day. It is always a short Bible verse — short enough to memorize easily so we can hold it before our minds all day. I, in my office, in bumper-to-bumper traffic, in my calling, and in counseling; my wife, at home, in shopping, and in answering the telephone; my children, in school and on the playground. No man is dressed to go out until he has dressed his mind with a fresh, clean, comfortable-fitting, protective idea.

4. Expose the brain to a constant positive diet. If you want something worthwhile to come out of your mind, you have to put something worthwhile into it. Cultivate the discriminatory art. Does this television program, this literature, this conversation inspire me? Am I feeding my mind a diet that will calm, challenge, uplift, or inject determination to go out and win? Go to the library and find books that will teach you more on the art of becoming a possibility thinker. There are many.

5. Give yourself an "in-depth" possibility-thinking treatment once a week. God knew what he was doing when he ordered the ancient Jews to reserve one day in seven for rest and worship. Find a place of religious worship that specializes in positive inspiration, and attend weekly. Often it's when you don't feel like going to church that you need it most. Your lack of desire for worship is a sure sign that you need inspiration, just as the unenthusiastic sputtering of a slowing car is a certain sign that it is running out of gas.

6. Talk yourself into possibility thinking. Affirm: "I can do all things through Christ who is strengthening me." You can talk yourself into almost any attitude.

Most of us have too often talked ourselves into fatigue, failure, and defeat. Repeat aloud, "I'm tired," "I'm finished," "I'm through" — and you will soon believe it.

Repeat the following sentences *out loud.* You will feel like a hypocrite, a braggart, and a liar. But read — out loud — then repeat again and again — *louder* — these powerful affirmations:

I can do great things.

I have great possibilities deep inside of me.

I have possibilities that haven't been born yet.

I'm really a wonderful person when Christ lives in me.

I've been too self-critical.

I've been my own worst enemy.

I'm a child of God. God loves me.

I can do all things through Christ who strengthens me.

Your biggest problem will be to believe it deeply enough to try it long enough and loudly enough to dehypnotize yourself from the mesmerizing power of your impossibility thinking.

7. *Use prayer power.* Try the prayer that Daniel Poling said three times every morning, as soon as he arose: "I believe. I believe. I believe!" This kind of prayer really flushes the negative out of the brain! Now repeat: "I can. I can. I can."

Ask God to help you to become a possibility thinker. Ask him once, and never again. Stop begging and start thanking. Thank him for hearing your prayer. Thank him for what he is doing about it. After all, God wants to see his sons and daughters walk with shoulders back, heads erect, with dignity shining in their faces.

8. *Have a thorough personality checkup.* Begin with a physical checkup. Then have a good spiritual checkup. How healthy is your faith? Healthy Christianity sets men free from the guilts, fears, worries, and anxieties that would feed feelings of indignity. Real Christianity tells us that we can really be somebody.

There were some tough, crude, unschooled fishermen who ran into a fellow years ago. He put his hand on their shoulders and said, "Follow me and I will make you fishers of men!" It was their moment of inspiration. When they were discouraged and felt they didn't amount to anything, he siad, "You are the salt of the earth . . . you are the light of the world." More than anything they knew that they could be persons in a world of nonpersons. That great inspirer was Jesus Christ. What a great possibility thinker! Draw close to him. Catch his spirit and you will never be the same again. Let Jesus Christ redesign your self-image.

Now let your imagination pull those great possibilities out of you.

LOSER'S LIMP?

"Watch this," chuckled an athletic coach as we watched his track team compete in a high school athletic meet. "You see my boy there, coming in fourth? Limping! Chances are he just developed that limp to have an excuse for not doing better. I call it loser's limp."

Some of the reasons why some men do not attain their goals — do not get one-tenth of the way to their goals — are no more convincing than the high school boy's suddenly developed limp. Worse yet, the loser's-limp attitude may stop a man from even trying to lift his life above a subsistence level. When the gun goes off to start the race, he is licked before he starts.

He may put it to you earnestly: "You can see how badly I am handicapped by . . ." and what follows is something defined as a handicap. Very rarely is it actually a handicap. Over and over, when some man tells me he is handicapped, I see a built-in loser's limp.

I am not talking about blind people, although one can still learn a wonderful lesson from Helen Keller. I am not talking about bedridden people, notwithstanding the fact that such men as James Royce, completely immobilized by polio, have built a thriving business from their beds. We should take off our hats to really handicapped people who still live constructive lives, but they are too exceptional for most of us to identify with.

I am talking, rather, about men who have the use of all their senses and all their limbs, surely the great majority of my readers.

And perhaps I speak directly to you — if you have never taken charge of your life-dynamics; if you know that many and many another man, who has nothing you haven't got, is building a grand career and a glorious future while you get pushed into some low-level corner. If you've lost a few of life's races, see if you're not assuming you're a loser forever, if you're not acquiring a loser's limp before you start.

Check yourself for loser's limp right now!

—J. K. SUMMERHILL

HOW TO MOTIVATE

by W. Clement Stone

President, Combined Insurance Company of America

Any man can be a success. He can become as rich as he wants, no matter how poor his start in life. I speak from experience.

I began my business career as a sixteen-year-old insurance salesman, calling door to door at the Dime Bank Building in Detroit. In four years' time, I had my own agency, begun with $100. Now I have my own insurance company with assets of more than $150 million.

To be a success, a man must program himself for it — just as a computer is programmed. In fact, a computer is just a poor imitation of that wonderful creature, man — a creature with an incomparable brain and a mind of indescribable powers.

There are three essential ingredients you must program into yourself for continued success.

The most important is *inspiration to action*. Inspiration to action means self-motivation, an inner urge that determines choice and incites us to action.

The other essential elements are *knowledge* and *know-how*. But the most important is inspiration to action.

How do you motivate yourself — or others — to action? With the magic ingredient. And here's what it is.

Some time ago, a rich cosmetic manufacturer retired. His products were fabulously successful. His friends badgered him for the secret of their success. Year after year, he jokingly refused. But finally he relented.

"In addition to the formulas that all cosmeticians use," he said, "I always added the magic ingredient to mine."

"What was that?"

"Well," he replied, "I never promised a woman that my products would make her beautiful, but I always gave her hope."

Hope, of course, *is the magic ingredient.* It is desire, with the belief that the goal is obtainable and with the expectation of reaching it.

You give yourself hope — you motivate yourself to action with what I call PMA — a Positive Mental Attitude.

There's a formula for generating that attitude of mind. Memorize, understand, and repeat frequently: "What the mind can conceive and believe, the mind can achieve." It's a form of self-suggestion, a self-motivator to success. When it becomes a part of you, you dare to aim higher.

There are other self-motivators that will spur us to action. You choose whatever motivators you need. You don't have to have many. Let's say that you procrastinate. To cure that bad habit, all you do is repeat fifty times in the morning and fifty times at night — and as often as you wish during the day: "Do it now; do it now; do it now."

Finally, it becomes part of your subconscious. Then, whenever you are tempted to put something off, that subliminal message will flash through your mind. And you'll act on it.

One of the most effective ways of motivating yourself — or others — is by reading inspirational, self-help books and articles. Take almost any man who has been phenomenally successful, and you'll find that somewhere along the line he was exposed to books like that. Napoleon Hill's *Think and Grow Rich* is one of the best. Another is William Danforth's *I Dare You*. So is *Success Through a Positive Mental Attitude,* which I wrote with Napoleon Hill.

Another effective way to motivate others is by example. Let me give an illustration from my own experience, one that also illustrates the power of a Positive Mental Attitude.

After I acquired my own insurance agency, I was training a salesman who had been working Sioux Center, Iowa. He was low. He had gone two days without making a sale.

"It's impossible to sell there," he said. "The people are Dutch and clannish. They won't buy from a stranger. Besides, they've had crop failures five times in a row."

So I suggested we drive to Sioux Center the next day and let me try. I wanted to prove to him that if he used my sales system and had a Positive Mental Attitude he could sell despite any obstacles.

On the way to Sioux Center, I closed my eyes, relaxed, and conditioned myself. I kept thinking why I could and should sell these people — rather than why I couldn't.

"He says they're Dutch and clannish and won't buy," I thought. "That's good. Everyone knows that if you can sell one in a clan, especially a leader, you can sell them all. Also, they've had bad crops. That's good, too. They're thrifty people, and save their money. Yet they want to protect their families and property.

"But they probably don't have any insurance, because most salesmen are too discouraged to tackle them. Now, our policies offer good protection at low cost, and I'll find no competition. So selling should be easy."

Then I engaged in what I call "mind-conditioning." I repeated over and over to myself, with reverence, sincerity, expectation, and emotion: "Please, God, help me sell." Then I took a nap, to arrive refreshed and ready to go.

The first place we called was a bank. Within twenty minutes, I sold the vice-president. Then I sold the cashier. From there, we began to cold-canvass — sell without appointment in every office and store in town. Everyone we called on that day bought a policy.

Why did I succeed where the other man failed? Because I knew and believed they would buy for the same reasons he was sure they wouldn't — because they were Dutch, clannish, and their crops had failed. Also, I had something more. And that was the difference between a negative mental attitude and PMA. I had asked for divine guidance and help. And what's more, I believed I was receiving it.

In addition to motivation and PMA, the successful man must have two other things working for him.

One is know-how — the quality that enables you to do something at will with skill, effectiveness, and a minimum use of time and effort. Know-how gets things done when people are wondering if they can be done. How do you get it? You don't get it — you accumulate it by doing, by action, by experience.

The other ingredient of success is knowledge. It's different from know-how. Knowledge for a salesman, for example, means complete information about the product or service he sells and how to sell it. It's something you can acquire from books, from the experience of others, and from those who are willing to teach. It's theory or abstract knowledge.

I've applied in my own life the principles of the success system that never fails.

I was sixteen when I sold my first insurance policy. We called on banks, offices, and stores during business hours. When a salesman calls door to door in an office building, there's always some feeling of timidity, which is a shade of fear. And if he's turned down, a salesman is pretty low.

I had the same feeling, and I had to find out how to overcome it. First, I spent a full day at the office reading and studying the policy I was to sell the next day and ways to sell it.

That's knowledge. Putting it into practice is know-how. Then comes Positive Mental Attitude.

After much thought, I reasoned: success is won by those who try. And where there's nothing to lose by trying, and a great deal to gain, by all means try.

Repeating this self-motivator over and over again would get me up to the door. But I was still timid about going in. Then I hit on the right self-starter: "Do it now!" And I found that action would dispel fear. Emotions are not subject to reason, but they're always subject to action. If you have butterflies in your stomach, and you're scared stiff, you can overcome fear at once by taking the right kind of action — by talking rapidly, loudly, emphasizing important words, pausing properly between phrases, keeping a smile in your voice and modulating it.

It works ninety-nine times out of a hundred.

Sales depend on the attitude of the salesman — not the attitude of the prospect. The salesman who is motivated and has the proper know-how and knowledge can influence his prospect to buy.

But how about motivating others? The same principles apply as in motivating ourselves. When I was a trustee of the Chicago Boys Club — I'm president now — our professional director told us we had a duty to share our talents with the boys. So I decided to form a Junior Success Club for them. There were two things they wanted to do. First, learn how to earn an honest dollar. Second, and this amazed me, they wanted to do better in school.

I went into detail to show that it takes less work to succeed than to fail, if you concentrate your energies or efforts. They learned the self-motivators and read the self-help books.

Then we taught them where to look for a job, how to sell themselves and how to leave pleasantly if they were turned down. Within thirty days, all sixteen kids had jobs.

Then we tackled the schoolwork. In ninety days we had youngsters who had jumped ahead two grades. But they had paid the price. These kids would spend an hour and a half every night to catch up. Some of them now have their master's degrees and are going for doctorates. Slum kids who — without motivation, know-how or knowledge — were going nowhere!

We also took convicts who wanted to straighten out their lives and applied the same principles.

First, we get the man to recognize that, as far as he is concerned, he's the most important person on earth. He has a brain, the same as everyone else, and that awesome power we're unable to define — the mind.

Furthermore, in his subconscious he has inherited from the vast reservoir of the past the power to do what those in the past have done.

Records were kept on eight hundred prisoners, chosen at random from Illinois penitentiaries, who took the course. Only 16 percent of them went back behind prison walls.

When you share what you have, what's left multiplies and grows. To succeed, you must become emotionally mature and see the broader horizons in life. You must become aware of the power of the individual to make this world a better place in which to live. And when you do that, happiness and wealth will follow.

Sense shines with a double luster when it is set in humility. An able and yet humble man is a jewel worth a kingdom.

—WILLIAM PENN

YOUR BODY — ASSET OR LIABILITY

by J. Allan Petersen

President, Family Concern

The Victorians were very sure that the human body must be treated with distrust, distaste, and disgust — as being without question the seat of sin.

Our Playboy contemporaries are equally sure that the human body is a toy — a plaything to be exposed and exploited, with selfish, cannibalistic greed — without regard to the human spirit within.

The average businessman thinks of his body as a machine to be driven to the limit of its endurance, simultaneously pouring into it alcohol, nicotine, pep pills, tranquilizers and a lot of groceries.

All of these attitudes are warped. Another man, David, king of Israel, had a very different philosophy. He exclaimed,

"You made all the delicate, inner parts of my body, and knit them together in my mother's womb. Thank you for making my body so wonderfully complex! It is amazing to think about. Your workmanship is marvelous — and how well I know it!" (Psalm 139:13, 14, TLB).

You see, the body was God's idea. He gave the first man a body, and every man since has come into the world in a body.

How do you feel about your body? Thankful? Resentful? Wishful? How do you treat your body? Respectfully? Creatively? Neglectfully? Indulgently? How you feel and what you do about this God-given vehicle may well represent your entire future. After all, the first impression anyone has of you is through either your voice or your body. You had better not ignore it — no one else is going to.

Furthermore, all your dreams — all the plans you have concerning your home, your family, your job, your position in life, your usefulness to your fellow man — all these are largely contingent upon the inner health and outward appearance of your body.

How you care for your physical well-being will largely depend on the importance you place on it. You would do well to look on your body in three primary ways: as an investment, as an instrument, and as an inheritance.

Your body is an investment. Since all that you accomplish in life will be done through your body, what a terrific investment you have in it! What a high value you must place upon it! Now, when you make an investment of any kind, you know that even a little put into a growing project on a long-range basis can bring multiplied dividends. And the greater the investment the more impressive the returns.

The farmer recognizes his land as his most indispensable investment. Consequently, he pours into its development thousands of dollars for machinery, fertilizer, insecticides, irrigation, seed, and hired help. From sunup to sundown, from early spring till the ground is frozen, his time goes into the working of that property. He obeys the laws of nature, planting at the proper time, rotating crops, resting a field, clearing the weeds, harvesting the ripened grain. To neglect his farm would inevitably result in bankruptcy.

These same laws must be followed by every man who takes his body seriously.

First, cultivating. The ground is hard and unresponsive. No farmer would waste seed on such soil. It must be broken up, stirred up by the plow, made ready to produce a crop. Many a man has let his body settle down into a similar condition. Stiff, unresponsive. Old before its time. What plowing is to the soil, exercise is to the body.

William Danforth, founder of the Ralston Purina Company, was a very frail child. Doctors agreed that he could not live long. But one of his teachers saw great possibilities in young William, and challenged him: "I dare you to be strong! I dare you to have a strong body, a strong mind and spirit." Something rose up in the boy, and he responded to the dare with everything in him. From that day on, step by step, he made himself into a strong, virile, healthy specimen of manhood. His life was full and abundant, and he lived to a ripe old age.

In *Treasury of Success Unlimited* (Hawthorn Books), we read that Dr. T. K. Cureton of the University of Illinois recommended a health program to a fifty-nine-year-old professor who complained of a number of ailments, including excess weight. The professor had been doing no regular exercise. After six months on the program, his abdominal fat was decreased 46 percent, his overall fat 28 percent, his blood pressure had dropped 20-41 percent. His weight had dropped only 2 percent, indicating that solid tissue had replaced flabbiness. His back and legs were much stronger, his chest expansion up 4 percent. Needless to say, his physical complaints had largely vanished.

Second, fertilizing and sowing. A farmer would indeed be foolish who, after sweating long hours in the burning sun to break up the hardened soil and prepare it for seed, would then apply a poor-grade fertilizer and low-germinating seed.

It has been said in many ways, "You are what you eat." It's an indisputable fact, and one we often ignore. A well-balanced diet, high in protein and supplemented as necessary by vitamins, is as essential to good health as proper exercise. The two should always go together. Dr. Cureton's program, as given to the professor, is as follows:

Walk two miles a day.

Perform calisthenics before breakfast and at bedtime.

Take a cool bath six days a week, a short hot bath on the seventh day, with a brisk towel rub after each.

Play golf or take a long hike once a week.

Eat fewer fried and starchy foods; more fruit, vegetables, and protein foods.

Third, rotating. Every farmer is well aware that to plant a field with the same crop year after year will soon deplete the soil and render it worthless. The ground needs to "rest."

"Since man first trod this earth," writes O. A. Battista, "his hours of darkness have been his hours of rest. Now, although he has learned to make artificial daylight, his twentieth-century body still refuses to function properly without sleep. Yet sleeplessness is fast becoming a major problem in our country, where more than five hundred tons of sleeping pills are sold each year."

He makes these practical suggestions:

"If you feel rested, you've had enough sleep.

A half-hour's nap equals three hours of night sleep.

Never wrestle with the day's problems or mull over your pleasant recollections — let everything go for the morrow.

Learn to think of sleep in terms of quality rather than quantity — a short but deep sleep does more for you than a long period of restless tossing and turning.

Learn to pull down the shade on your mind and shut out the day's doings — a half-hour before bedtime, stop anything you may be doing that requires mental effort."

Considering you spend one-third of your life in bed, sleep is a matter worthy of your most conscientious efforts.

Your body is an instrument. The farmer must keep the instruments of his labor free from rust. The doctor's instrument must be sharp and sterile. The instrument of the scientist — his mind — must be kept alert, perceptive, free of anything that might fog it. And the instrument of the athlete — of any man — his body, should be clean, uncorrupted, and disciplined.

The Apostle Paul puts it this way: "In a race, everyone runs, but only one person gets first prize. So run your race to win. To win the contest, you must deny yourselves many things that would keep you from doing your best. An athlete goes to all this trouble just to win a blue ribbon or a silver cup, but we do it for a heavenly reward that never disappears. So I run straight to the goal with purpose in every step. I fight to win. I'm not just shadow-boxing or playing around. Like an athlete, I punish my body, treating it roughly, training it to do what it should, not what it wants to. Otherwise, I fear that after enlisting others for the race, I myself might be declared unfit and ordered to stand aside" (1 Corinthians 9:24-27, TLB).

What Paul is speaking of here, of course, is self-discipline.

An undisciplined horse is of no value to the farmer. An undisciplined child may become a menace to society. An undisciplined athlete never reaches the top.

Dr. Harry J. Johnson, president of Life Extension Foundation, calls over-eating America's number-one health hazard. Most of us have fallen into the undisciplined habit of feeding our appetite, not our hunger.

"I refuse to do what I think might get such a grip on me that I can't easily stop when I want to. Take the matter of eating. God has given us an appetite for food and stomachs to digest it, but that doesn't mean we should eat more than we need" (1 Corinthians 6:12, 13, TLB).

As Dr. Frederick Stare, the Harvard nutritionist, puts it, "Overweight results not from what you eat and drink between Christmas and New Year's but from what you eat and drink between New Year's and Christmas."

Let's talk about what you drink. It is estimated that about one of fifteen people in the U. S. will end up as an alcoholic, usually without realizing that he was walking into disaster. What causes that one to step into the abyss? There is no total agreement among the experts. But of one thing there can be no doubt: the man who refrains from drinking alcohol will never become an alcoholic. The *Journal of the American Medical Association* says, "Drink has taken five million men and women in the U. S., taken them as masters take slaves, and new acquisitions are going on at the rate of 200,000 a year." As a very conservative estimate, assume that each alcoholic affects the lives of at least three other persons, children and spouses, whose lives become warped, twisted, out of focus. The number of victims directly and indirectly affected sky-rockets into the twenty million bracket.

And what about smoking? The report of the Surgeon General of the U. S. Public Health Service has convinced most people of the danger of smoking. But nothing dies harder than old habits, and the most stubborn of these seems to be smoking, though 100,000 doctors have quit with good reason. The evidence piling up higher every year abundantly proves that the two biggest killers in America, heart disease and cancer, are definitely linked with smoking. Comparing the smoker and the nonsmoker, lung cancer occurs eight times more often in a person who smokes only a pack a day. Coronary heart disease is found fifty percent more often in men who smoke. Is it worth it?

In *Sin, Sex, and Self-Control,* Norman Vincent Peale tells of one who gave up both smoking and drinking. "Every time I took a drink or lit a cigarette, I asked myself this question: 'Are you gaining control, or losing it?' It was pretty obvious to me that after one drink I had less power of choice. I was losing control, not gaining it. As for cigarettes, when I felt a strong urge to light one and gave in to that urge, I was surrendering my freedom of choice again. I finally decided that life is complicated enough without these petty tyrants interfering with your freedom and pushing you around. So I made up my mind to get rid of them altogether, and I did!"

Peale summarizes our subject in this way: "Discipline is the price you pay for freedom. It is a liberator; it sets you free — free from the tyranny of laziness, of sloth, of flabbiness — physical and mental, of harmful habits. Discipline restores your freedom of choice."

Your body is an inheritance. It was given to you as a trust from a wise, loving God. You will someday stand before that Creator and give an account of what you have done with that trust. "For we shall all stand before the Judgment Seat of Christ . . . that everyone may receive the things done in his *body,* according to that he hath done, whether it be good or bad" (2 Corinthians 5:10).

Discipline in these body habits is very important. A man may be very well controlled in his diet, take pride in a strong body, and wisely shun alcohol and tobacco. However, this is not enough. He may be practicing the only thing that God expressly calls "the sin against his body."

"Sexual sin is never right. Our bodies were not made for that, but for the Lord, and the Lord wants to fill our bodies with himself. . . . That is why I say to run from sex sin. No other sin affects the body as this one does. When you sin this sin it is against your own body. Haven't you yet learned that your body is the home of the Holy Spirit God gave you? Your body does not belong to you, for God bought you with a great price . . . If anyone defiles and spoils God's home, God will destroy him. For God's home is holy and clean, and you are that home" (1 Corinthians 6:13b, 18-20; 3:17, TLB).

Certainly there is nothing wrong with sex. It is the fabulous gift of God, ordained for the propagation of the race, marital pleasure, and the expression of that kind of love between man and wife which nourishes true oneness. God protects love by confining sex to marriage, for marriage provides love its best opportunity to develop and mature. Sex destroys when it operates outside the plan for marriage, while sex relationships practiced within this plan make life rich and complete. The Song of Solomon reveals the kind of healthy appreciation of the human body that God intended within marriage.

But every good gift God has given has been degraded by man for his own selfish ends. If you were an animal, you would live on the level of instinct and satisfy your sexual cravings with any other animal at any time. But being made in the image of God, you cannot live that way and escape secret guilt or find the fulfillment you really want.

God's warning that "sexual sin is never right" is for our own protection. It is in the Bible because it is true, true to the very nature of the universe and of man. It is the only thing that really works. So if a man decides to use his body dishonorably, he is in conflict with himself. The moral breakdown results in an inward breakdown, and this moral decay can reach such a point where God gives men up "to be the playthings of their own foul desires in dishonoring their own bodies" (Romans 1:24, Phillips).

"A body hast thou prepared me," Jesus said to his Father, and every man can say the same. Christ cherished and nourished his body, caring for it wisely, and using it sacrificially in the service of God. He is no longer on earth in his own body, but he walks and works through other bodies that possess the Holy Spirit. Your body is valuable — cherish it. Your body is powerful — control it. Your body can be God's instrument — give it.

"And so . . . I plead with you to give your bodies to God. Let them be a living sacrifice, holy — the kind he can accept. When you think of what he has done for you, is this too much to ask?" (Romans 12:1, TLB).

"Alcoholism is a disease? If so, it is the only disease that is contracted by an act of the will. It is the only disease that requires a license to propagate it. It is the only disease that is bottled and sold. It is the only disease that promotes crime. It is the only disease that is habit-forming. It is the only disease that is spread by advertising. It is the only disease that is given for a Christmas present."

—PETER L. REAM

MARK IT "MATURITY"

by Richard Shelley Taylor

Professor, Nazarene Theological Seminary
Kansas City, Missouri

The term "discipline" carries a variety of meanings. To the child it means being compelled to do something undesirable and being punished if he rebels. To the soldier, discipline means conformity to regulations, instant obedience to orders, K.P. duty, reveille on cold mornings. To the student it means the course of instruction he is undertaking, with the specific requirements and rules and examinations incident to it. To the Christian, discipline means discipleship — following Jesus, with one's self denied and one's cross resolutely carried.

But there is something more. The aim of discipline is a disciplined character which goes beyond the minimum demands of these specific disciplines and permeates the whole life. It is possible for the Christian to be a sincere and regenerated follower of Jesus yet remain undisciplined in many areas of life.

In a general sense, self-discipline is the ability to regulate conduct by principle and judgment rather than impulse, desire, high pressure, or social custom. It is basically the ability to subordinate.

APPETITES

There are several aspects here. For one thing, there is the ability to subordinate the body and its physical appetites to the service of the mind. Paul said, "I keep my body under." This was exemplified by a fellow preacher who became convinced that coffee was affecting his heart — a Norwegian, mind you, who had enjoyed coffee all his life! "But," he said, "that moment it became a matter of conscience with me. So I stopped." Just that simple. He hasn't touched it since.

The subordination of the physical includes not only the

appetite for food but also the sex urge. In some this has been so indulged that it is abnormally excitable. To make matters worse, such persons often live by the creed of weakness: "I can't help it," and similar expressions of moral flabbiness. Overindulgence even within marriage may have the effect of cultivating this basic urge until it is increasingly imperious in its demands. Those so afflicted are in grave danger of succumbing to temptation from outside marriage when domestic stress, "frigidity" in their mates, long illness, or separations subject their enfeebled powers of self-control to an abnormal strain.

Too often the moral downfall of men is blamed on some failure in their wives. That is a cowardly evasion of moral responsibility. The man of disciplined character does not have to have a warm, responsive wife, who caters to his every impulse, to keep him in the path of virtue. He keeps himself there, by the grace of God. If his relationship with his wife is happy, he is grateful; if it is not, he simply appropriates more grace, and demonstrates the man that he is. A weak man is a poor risk no matter how warm his wife is; a strong man will keep himself pure even if it means total abstinence the rest of his life. And it must be affirmed emphatically that this is not just a matter of being "made that way" or natural temperament; it is a matter of achieving complete subordination.

Many marriages are less than ideal in their physical aspects. So what? Must there therefore be irritability, constant tension, and perpetual teetering on the brink of moral infidelity? Such un-ideal conditions are often the rock on which the marriage is built into a stronger and finer edifice. In these very problems a couple may find a deeper meaning of love and a truer, richer stability. They become gentler, nobler, spiritually taller. The marriage is not just "saved"; it is often stronger than marriages wherein there have been no deep struggles and decisive conquests.

EMOTIONS

Again, emotions must be subordinate to the reason. The

heart needs to be first cleansed, then kept on the leash of discipline. An unmarried Christian man may develop a friendship with an unregenerate woman at the office or at school or in some other perfectly natural and legitimate relationship. At first there is no thought of love. In fact, the Christian may even be motivated by an honest desire to help the other spiritually. But if the two are thrown more and more together, gradually there may steal into their hearts that which lights the eye and quickens the pulse at the other's presence. Then the Christian will have to face a terrible emotional struggle to become extricated or an unscriptural marriage will result.

An even more dangerous peril can exist in male-female friendships between married Christians. Their work (even the Lord's work) may legitimately throw them into each other's company. Such friendships may be holy and beautiful on a brother-sister basis. But a certain reserve and distance must be preserved at all costs, and will be by men and women of disciplined character. Friendship can become affection, affection love, love lust, and the progress be a shock to both. That which began innocently may end disastrously.

The rugged advice of Jesus to pluck out the offending eye, or cut off the hand or foot, is never more apropos than in this kind of situation. Souls, homes, happiness, influence — all will be saved only by drastic, even ruthless, action. The feelings must not be spared. Here again Christians must tolerate not the least vestige of the philosophy of weakness: "I can't help it." Emotions may not immediately obey the will, but actions must. In due course, by the grace of God, emotions will follow the lead of disciplined adjustment, strong purpose, and decisive stand.

The finest discipline of all does not struggle out of a near-tragic situation, but it foresees and forestalls the situation in the first place. The young Christian who adopts certain basic principles respecting friendships and avoids making intimate alliances with the unsaved will not have the battle with tumultuous desires and affections later on. And the married Christian worker who is alert to the perils which beset him and is self-disciplined always in look and word and action will not ignite fires which he will have to fight feverishly to put out.

MOODS

Disciplined character also means the mastery of moods. This is yet another area of conquest in the subordination of one's emotions. A tendency to exhibit moodiness is a grave weakness. The mature person learns to apply himself to the regular tasks of life with a consistent "face" in spite of varying moods.

It is said that a Christian once asked Amanda Smith what she should do when a cloud settled down over her spirit. The black saint replied, "What do you do when you are setting the table and a shadow falls across the room?"

The lady answered, "I just take a quick look to see if a serious storm is brewing, and if not I go right on setting the table."

"Do exactly the same," admonished Mrs. Smith. "When a cloud comes over your soul, take a quick look to see if sin has brought darkness. If you find no sin, just go right on setting the table for the Lord." That is mastering our moods. That, too, is growing up.

SPEECH

Regardless of how carefully controlled a person is at all other points, none can qualify for the high rating of a truly disciplined character whose tongue is not restrained by the bridle of prudence and directed by the reins of love.

Some people pride themselves on their frankness. "I say what I think," they boast. So does the fool, according to the Bible: "A fool uttereth all his mind." Frankness is indeed a virtue when coupled with intelligent, loving tact and discretion. But it becomes a sadistic vice when it is merely the unbridled eruptings of opinions without regard to times and places or human feelings. It often takes a far higher display of discipline to refrain from speaking than it does to speak. Forbearance is a Christian virtue, even as is frankness.

PRIORITIES

Furthermore, a truly disciplined character has the ability to subordinate the lesser to the greater. Here is the problem of priorities — probably the most crucial problem of life. On its solution hang success or failure, improvement or degeneration, and in the larger sense, heaven or hell.

This involves ability to reject day by day that great army of possible activities which clamor for our precious energy but which would hamper the doing of more important things. If our lives are to be fruitful and purposeful, we must heroically and decisively put the knife to most of the possible activities which could clutter every single day.

Now we must say "yes" to this and "no" to that. Now we must put first things first. It is reported that when a professional author said to Sir Winston Churchill that he couldn't write unless the "mood" came on him, the great statesman replied: "No! Shut yourself in your study from nine to one and make yourself write. Prod yourself! Kick yourself! It's the only way."

ADJUSTMENT TO AUTHORITY

The final hallmark of the disciplined character is the ability to assimilate imposed discipline with grace and profit. Rebellion at times may be one's clear duty. But in most of life's normal relationships rebellion is stupid and destructive. Being a constitutional rebel is no ground for pride. Habitual rebellion is the cult of weaklings rather than the strong. It requires neither intelligence nor character to assert loudly, "No one can tell me what to do." But it requires both to submit to the inescapable and necessary constraints of society and to submit, not grudgingly, but graciously, with mature understanding and cheerful good will.

Christians must find their way between extreme nonconformity and extreme subjugation. They must learn to draw the line before proper subjection extinguishes private thinking and personal initiative. Insubordination is bad, but individuality is good.

It takes careful thinking to discriminate between distortion and normalcy in all of these facets of Christian discipline. But the essential fact is clear: discipline is the mark of maturity. Without discipline the character will remain weak and infantile.

Take time for work; it is the price of success.
Take time to think; it is the source of power.
Take time to play; it is the secret of youth.
Take time to read; it is the foundation of wisdom.
Take time to be friendly; it is the road to happiness.
Take time to dream; it's hitching your wagon to a
*   star.*
Take time to love; it is the highest joy of life.
Take time to laugh; it is the music of the soul.

—ANONYMOUS

2

The Man and His Marriage

MAN, THE LEADER

by David W. Augsburger

Radio Speaker, The Mennonite Hour

What is leadership in the home?

There is the "man-is-and-ever-shall-be-the-sole-leader" theory. This view assumes that some superior gift of chromosomes and hormones makes man the natural possessor of unique talents and abilities which fit him to lead out. He is, due to his strength, size, intelligence, and tendency toward dominance, naturally "the boss."

Dominance may effectively give orders and demand control, but it does not lead. Dominant authority serves well as a censor, an enforcer of views, a dispenser of discipline. But that is not leading.

And dominance is not uniquely characteristic of either sex. It is often an evidence of a rigid, authoritative personality. Frequently it is a sign of weakness and insecurity, indicating that the domineering person fears change or challenge so greatly that he/she cannot risk being flexible and is terrified of becoming vulnerable before another personality.

There is the "husband-is-the-head-and-the-head-is-the-leader" theory. The husband may be the "head," but to be head and to be leader are two different things. Headmanship is not synonymous with leadership. The headman may serve as the formal "chief-in-charge," as the recognized "legal name and nominal head" (as does the husband, whose family name becomes the title for social use). But such "headmanship" is much more than a matter of status, rank, or recognition. It accepts the responsibility for failures and successes in the relationship, but does not assume sole authority in decisions and directions.

Nor does the biblical recognition of man as "head" in marriage endow him with authority and right-to-dominate. Some have thought that Paul's patterning of man's role as "head" after Christ's position as "head-of-the-church" gives great weight to the husband's role.

Does the husband, like Christ, become lord and master? The ultimate word? Since the two, man and Christ, are compared, does that give man all the rights and roles of lord in the home? On the contrary, the purposes of the comparison are specifically stated (in both 1 Corinthians 11:1-10, and Ephesians 5:21-33). Headship means responsibility and initiative: responsibility to act in love; initiative to act in service. As Christ acted in self-giving love and self-humbling service (giving us a whole new meaning to "headship"), so husbands take the initiative in building an atmosphere of loving, self-sacrificing service.

Headmanship is only part of leadership, one facet of one kind of leadership.

Christ cut through our contorted ideas of headship with surgical words: "Among the heathen it is their kings who lord it over them, and their rulers are given the title of 'benefactors.' But it must not be so with you! Your greatest man must become like a junior and your leader must be a servant. Who is the greater, the man who sits down to dinner or the man who serves him? Obviously, the man who sits down to dinner — yet I am the one who is the servant among you" (Luke 22:25-27, Phillips).

Leadership is accepting responsibilities and performing certain functions in a marriage relationship in a way that advances both together toward their goals.

If leadership is "doing certain tasks or functions," then it is obviously not a certain role, a certain sex, or a permanent possession of one of the persons. Leadership alternates; it is a contribution made by either or both together.

If leadership is "helping and serving so that both move forward," then it is an action done by either person in a way that liberates both. It may go unnoticed. It happens best when unrecognized. It is accepted most easily when it is unselfconscious, selfless, self-giving, when it is exercised in the Christ-way of giving help.

Helping another is best defined as giving another the freedom to change, and change voluntarily. This is a creative exercise in leadership. In contrast, authoritarian dominance prohibits free choice, and inhibits free interchange and the freedom to change.

The autocratic personality	*The Christ-ocratic personality*
gives orders without asking questions, without permitting questions; makes demands, dishes out directives, lays down the law, is defensive if challenged; requires compliance regardless of consent or agreement; pushes and manipulates one-man rule in over-under position; says "You do, you must do, you ought to have done, you'd better do"; depends on his own external authority to motivate others; generates friction, resistance,	asks questions, seeks to truly hear, suggests alternatives; respects freedom and dignity of others, can affirm the truth clearly and concretely but nondefensively; values willing cooperation, works for open agreement and understanding; leads, attracts, persuades personal relationships in side-by-side identification; says, "Come, let's do, we might have done, can we try?" depends on their internal integrity to motivate them; generates acceptance, cooperation, and

resentment;	reconciliation;
separates and	unites and helps persons
isolates people.	relate to each other.

Marriage partners tend to become like each other, taking on the other's qualities, or developing the opposite characteristics in negative reaction to the other.

Leadership shared in mutual respect can establish a climate of dignity, freedom, and responsibility, creating an atmosphere which is both comforting and stimulating to both — a Christian atmosphere. In it, each is free to grow toward personal maturity and each is eager to see the shape of Christ forming in the other (see Galatians 4: 19, 20).

But where one seizes power, or both struggle for control, an atmosphere of competition and conflict chokes communication and understanding. Even the unconscious assuming of power by one partner or the other will mold the relationship, perhaps in ways neither desire.

Leadership is a function which should always be shared.

Authority in one area or another is a responsibility which is mutually designated to one or the other through honest negotiation. It can be renegotiated at any time.

Life together is life shared. Shared love, shared work, shared opportunities, shared leadership, even shared initiative. Man, the nominal head, may function officially for both in public matters of leadership. Woman, recognized as his equal in partnership, leads with, and not against him. Together, they choose to grow.

> To be a man
>> Is to possess the strength to love another,
>> Not the need to dominate over others.
>
> To be a man
>> Is to experience the courage to accept another,
>> Not the compulsion to be an aggressor.
>
> To be a man
>> Is to keep faith with human values in relationships,

Not to value oneself by position or possessions.
To be a man
  Is to be free to give love
  And to be free to accept love in return.

THIS IS LOVE

by Theodor Bovet, M.D.

Swiss physician and marriage counselor

When we speak of love we must distinguish between three different aspects of it. Unfortunately, these are often confused with or opposed to each other. Just as every human personality has a physical, a psychological, and a spiritual aspect (or dimension), so within the living organism or union of two persons in marriage there are three aspects — sex, *eros,* and *agape.*

The physical aspect is known as "sex." This comprises all the directly biological functions and experiences, from fertilization to birth.

Sexuality is a self-centered activity. It does, of course, transcend individuality in so far as it aims at propagation, for which it requires someone of the opposite sex, but its immediate motive is egoistic — the satisfaction of lust, sensual desire. The other person is only a means to an end, a person whose feelings are not taken into account.

It would be a mistake to try to use these facts to discredit sexuality, which carries out the task of procreation and is, therefore, as much a part of creation and just as much willed by God as the functions of digestion, respiration, and the circulation of the blood. But like these it is a part of a greater whole, and there is something unnatural about it when it is excited and experienced purely for its own sake.

Eros, unlike sex, is concerned with the other person as a person. It is not woman in general who attracts a man erotically, but some particular woman with her own personal characteristics.

Eros does all it can to bring out the specifically masculine or feminine characteristics of the personality. Grace and kindness, charm and delicacy on the one side; chivalry, courage, gentlemanly behavior, and attentiveness on the other; all these are, in the best sense of the word, erotic things.

Eros, being an activity of the human spirit, always implies a relationship between two people. It never aims at satisfying individual desire but at producing a relationship in which each will give pleasure to the other. Self-satisfaction is a feature of sex, which is a solitary thing; but *eros* is never solitary, for it lives by partnership. *Eros* finds its fulfillment in the relationship of love. It gives pleasure to both partners at the same time, enables them to give themselves to each other, entering into each other, stilling their own egos for the sake of each other.

It is one of the great misfortunes of our age that *eros* is largely unknown and confused with sexuality, at least in the case of men. Most of what is commonly described as erotic is merely sexual, and even the things that many moralists condemn as erotic are sexual too. In a certain hush-hush type of moral teaching, young men are left to fight their impulses alone and as a result never progress beyond the notion of love as a mere sexual impulse. What they need is to be educated beyond sex and up to *eros*. They need to be shown that the object of their main interest — a woman's body — though not in itself by any means evil or unimportant, is far less interesting than is a woman as a whole person: body, mind, and spirit.

The commonest infirmity in marriage is probably the underdevelopment of *eros*. Most husbands are prodigies in sex but almost complete morons so far as *eros* is concerned. And so their wives, who live more by *eros* than by sex, become psychologically disillusioned and, therefore, physically repelled by their husbands. Sexual coldness — "frigidity" as it is called — in wives is an exact reflection of a nonerotic and merely sexual attitude on the part of their husbands, and can only be cured by treating the latter first.

Water pipes only work at full pressure when the sluices are in proper order, and the maximum electric current can be maintained only when the whole circuit is properly insulated. If a short circuit occurs — i.e., when there is no resistance to the flow of current — the power quickly falls to zero. *Eros* depends in exactly the same way on the mastery of physical sex.

Young men — and older men too — must realize that they must control their impulses, not because these are bad things in themselves or that a lot of sexual activity might have serious physical consequences for them, but because they must keep the erotic tension high if they and their wives are to get the most out of it. Moral exhortations denouncing the sexual impulse express a fundamentally wrong point of view, and their effect upon young people is nil anyway. What these young people actually need to do is to learn the "art of love" as a thing willed by God. And in this matter, as in all others, there can be no art without discipline.

Love also has a third, spiritual aspect, which for want of a better name I must call *agape*. Sex has its center of gravity in the ego; *eros* has its center of gravity in "us two" — the human couple; *agape's* center of gravity lies beyond the human couple. *Agape* includes mutual responsibility, but also a further responsibility to a third party. It maintains loyalty between couples even when one party no longer desires to be loyal. "Fall but in love with me, loyal thou needst not be," sings *eros*. But *agape* knows that even in the best marriages there can be times when love ebbs and loyalty has to fill the gap.

Agape, as Brunner says, loves the other because he exists, not because of certain characteristics. A man loves his wife, not just her beautiful face; a woman loves her husband, not just his intellect. Thus *agape* is not tied to sexual differentiation like sex and *eros*. "There is no more male nor female, but all are one in Christ Jesus." So, too, *agape* is the basis of friendship. As Montaigne said of his friend LaBoëtie, "If I am bound to say why I loved him, I feel that the only answer I can give is — because he was he, and I was I."

But it would be a gross mistake to set up *agape* and

eros against each other as two mutually exclusive opposites, or as though *agape* was nobler and more "Christian" than *eros*. Both are necessary elements in any good marriage. Every good marriage must be a friendship as well as a marriage. Husband and wife must think as much of each other, love each other, interest each other, just as much as two really good friends. But woe to the marriage that is only a friendship, only *agape!* In every good marriage, too, husband and wife must love each other as passionately, go on making each other as happy, go on being as new a surprise to each other, as any pair of lovers who are "mad about each other." But woe to the marriage that is only passion, only *eros!*

Marriage begins when a man and woman decide to spend their lives together and make a public announcement of the fact. But as yet it is like a newborn child — a real person, but weak and in need of development. It takes years to develop fully. Like a child, too, it is not simply an assemblage of a number of parts — sex, *eros, agape,* loyalty, etc; it is a whole from the very beginning. But it grows with every day and goes on developing, as God intended it to.

Husband and wife share enjoyable experiences and frightening ones; they share drudgery and ecstasy. A child is given to them: they stand in amazement by its cradle, and later when it takes its first step from its mother's to its father's arms. Then again they bend over it together when it is ill; it pants for breath, and the same terror grips them and their joint prayer rises to God. If one of them is ill, the other does the work of both; if unemployment comes, they learn to economize and discover ways of dealing with the situation together.

At times, too, husband and wife come into conflict with each other. They cannot understand each other or put themselves in the other's place, or give way: harsh words are spoken and they both feel terribly lonely and miserable and bad-tempered. And then they discover that no one else can help them, and that they are each other's hearth and home; and they come together again, and are ashamed of their thick-skinned egoism, and throw another layer of it away, once and for all. Marriage grows with every sacred stirring that husband and wife feel together — out in the country, it may be, or listening to music, or reading the Bible — and with every kind word spoken in bad moments, and every burst of childish laughter.

Husband and wife share not only the past but the future too — their joint plans and hopes and anxieties, and the joint uncertainty of not knowing at morning whether they will be together again at evening. God holds them together in his hand. Such is marriage, and it is indissoluble.

This love, this bond, is used again and again in the Bible as the only simile adequate to express God's love of man and his covenant with his people. "As a young man marrieth a virgin, so shall thy sons marry thee: and as the bridegroom rejoiceth over the bride, so shall thy God rejoice over thee."

Thus married love has the power to make God's love either credible or incredible. Married love and fidelity decide what picture the wife or husband forms of God's love and fidelity.

He drank coffee to excess and I liked to stay up without it. I was economical, he insouciant about expenses. I forgot to turn out the lights and he put off writing letters. Little things like that. And you know what? We reformed each other — we both began to be dilatory together. It was wonderful how friction vanished once we had enough faults in common.

—PHYLLIS McGINLEY

YOUR WIFE'S PSYCHOLOGIST

by Paul Plattner, M.D.

Psychiatrist, Berne, Switzerland

In his depth every man harbors a strong, irresistible need for complementation, for fulfillment for the "other half." The sexual-erotic difference between marriage partners involves, of course, a great deal more than the difference in their sexual organs or their different tasks in connection with begetting children. Nevertheless, these bodily differences themselves are a particularly conspicuous expression of the incompleteness of the individual. In order to bring to birth a child, which is something new, something that points beyond the individual, cooperation of the true whole is necessary. And this applies to the physical as well as to the psychological dimension.

What are the respective sexual-erotic orientations of man and woman? How do they experience their sexuality, and how does it operate in their everyday existence rather than just in the brief moments of bodily union?

Man's sexual tension rises from a neutral point zero suddenly and to a very high level. It rapidly achieves its highest intensity and demands release. When release is obtained, a man quickly descends once again to a sexual-erotic zero point. And there he remains until a new, brusque ascent occurs. Between these peaks, man is, as it were, "empty of love" for a longer or shorter time. During such a neutral interim, he is relatively free erotically. In this phase, therefore, he is able to concentrate on factual or spiritual matters, to take an interest in things from which sexual love is wholly excluded. For example, he will engage in scientific work, solve intellectual or technical problems, in short, pursue his occupation. And this he is able to do without any regard whatever for his wife, entirely absorbed and fulfilled in his vocation, his work.

The expression "without regard" may be taken quite

literally in this case, in that he will hardly cast a glance in the direction of his wife, whereas she, who wants to be noticed more than anything else, will fare rather ill under such treatment. For she depends very much on the attention and consideration of her husband. If he pays no attention to her she will find him inconsiderate, and cruelly so.

The love graph of a woman follows an entirely different design. Once her love is awakened, it remains ever wakeful. She never sinks all the way to that zero point. For a woman, love is here to stay. It rises more gradually toward its peak, and, upon release, its descent is also more gradual. But it never descends as far as does the love graph of a man. A woman's erotic feeling is always present, at least to a degree. Therefore there is nothing purely objective, purely scientific, purely businesslike for her. Whatever she does, she does it always for her husband or for her children or for other people. It is for them she cooks, cleans, washes, mends clothes. It is for them that she decorates herself and her home. Therefore she cannot really understand why her husband does not respond to this love, why he hardly even notices her. It is very natural for her to talk often about her love, to ask her husband anxiously, "Do you still love me?" This sad question expresses her astonishment at the fact that her husband is able, at certain times, to exist without love, that at times he is, as it were, absent from this love, that he is able to be cool and objective.

The difference which we have just described appears in countless everyday marital difficulties. It leads to tensions and, if the partners do not recognize the fundamental nature of the difference, to a feeling of misunderstanding which puts a heavy burden upon the marriage. Let us illustrate with a very ordinary example.

On a certain morning the husband has a brief exchange of words with his wife over some trifle before he leaves for work. When he comes home for lunch, the atmosphere is calmer but harmony has not yet been clearly and consciously restored. At night he comes home from work in a very good mood. He is in high spirits, amiable, affectionate toward his wife. He has long since forgotten the little morning incident. In the course of the evening he wants to have intimate contact with his wife, but he encounters a resistance which he finds wholly incomprehensible and wounding.

Why does his wife remain cool or downright negative? Why does she not allow herself to be infected by his good mood and inner satisfaction? What has come over her, anyway? These are questions the husband asks himself, and from his standpoint he seems to be quite right.

The woman is in such cases similarly amazed at her husband's conduct. More precisely, his conduct saddens her because this scene has been played so often that she has ceased being amazed. But she still cannot understand how her husband can be so indifferent and loveless. How is it possible that he should have forgotten what happened this morning? The woman feels and thinks, "That argument of this morning is still between us; something more has to be done about it to restore harmony."

From the husband's point of view, the wife's feelings appear petty: she is far too sensitive, too easily bruised. After all, he has been friendly and affectionate. He has proved by his speech and actions that the morning incident has become a thing of the past. For him, feelings are not so important and decisive.

But this is not enough for his wife, and this is rather typical of women. The relationship of love which was disturbed in the morning has not yet been restored. And she cannot get over her sense of disharmony simply. It is impossible for her to consent truly to sexual union as long as marital harmony is lacking. The husband thinks that sexual union is the very thing that will take care of whatever residue of disharmony there may be. For his wife, however, such a notion is incomprehensible. She is unable to give herself unreservedly to her husband as long as she does not feel spiritually at one with him; and for that she needs at least a little talk about the incident of the morning. Any attempt to restore sexual togetherness before recovering their emotional erotic unity strikes her as crude, indeed as animalistic. Above all, she disapproves of the incomprehensible indifference of her husband who demonstrates in his conduct so little awareness of her feminine nature, which demands that he take such incidents with due seriousness.

The different way in which a man and a woman experience life colors their entire marriage. For the man, sexual union is an event with a significance of its own, having its own independent experiential value. Through sexual intercourse, he is able to recover community after having spent some time in a certain emotional isolation, a certain erotic neutrality, for example, after the day's work. This feeling of belonging, restored by the sexual event, he now takes with him joyfully and proceeds to discharge in his work the energy he has accumulated from being with his wife. He is now able to perform with heightened creativity and new zest because his work now seems ever so much more meaningful to him. It is for this reason that a man is able to attribute a spiritual meaning to sexual union, indeed a metaphysical significance.

The woman's story is entirely different. For the feminine soul, sexual union is both less and more. It is something very close and palpable. Her spiritual surrender is directed far more precisely at the person of her husband, perhaps at the hoped-for child. A woman expects every sexual union to bring her closer to her husband and to remain closer to him ever after.

An hour of peaceful togetherness in which the woman knows that her husband is really beside her, an hour during which he really participates in everything she tells him and he tells her, is likely to mean a great deal more to most women than any stormy sexual encounter during which she loves her husband, to be sure, but in which her husband actually gives himself to the experience rather than to his wife.

Insofar as a man is rather directly excitable, he is likely to interpret his wife's need to cling to him, her groping for friendliness and protection, as heralds of sexual activity. But for the woman this does not by any means follow. Her need for tenderness may be wholly free from sexual desire, so free indeed that she may recoil in fright when she senses that her husband is responding with sexual desire. Both husband and wife ought to acquaint themselves with these fundamental differences between men and women if they would avoid constant misunderstandings.

C. J. Jung comments: "Most men are erotically blind in that they commit the unpardonable error of confusing eros with sexuality. A man thinks that he possesses a woman when he is possessing her sexually. But never is he possessing her less, because for the woman only the erotic relationship is truly significant. For her, marriage is a relationship, and sexuality an addendum."*

For a man, the most significant thing in life is his work, his objective accomplishment. His work emerges gradually in some permanent and lasting form, and he feels himself affirmed by his creation. This feeling is clearly and understandably expressed in his professional pride. In addition, he expects material recognition of his work in the form of money.

For a woman, especially for a housewife, the situation is as a rule very different. Her devotion to her work appears in the form of clean, well-scrubbed children and a husband in neat, well-cared-for clothes, in the form of loving care for these and other persons. Unlike her husband, she does not normally receive any external recognition for her work in the form of regular pay. Nevertheless, she also has a quite natural need to be appreciated and to have her efforts and worries met with understanding. And this is something which men seldom realize. Time and again, a husband could cheer up his wife with just a few friendly, appreciative words. He could help her to enjoy or at least to endure her often thankless housework.

This entirely legitimate but often unfulfilled desire for

*C. J. Jung, *Women in Europe* (Zurich: Rascher, 1932)

some recognition is a frequent, unconscious source of marital disturbances. If a woman does not feel adequately understood and appreciated, she will be tempted to compensate for the missing understanding by provoking the attention, if not the esteem, of her husband. If her positive accomplishments cannot induce her husband to turn toward her, if the care of her beauty no longer entices him from his world into her world, she will often seek other means to establish contact with him.

Many scenes and "acts" which husbands usually put down with a contemptuous wave of the hand as feminine theatrics have to be judged and treated from this viewpoint. So does much steady complaining about fatigue, headaches, migraines, dizziness, backaches, and abdominal cramps. Such complaints and ailments are simple signals — signals to the man. They mean: "Don't leave me to myself! Pay attention to me! Understand me! Be near me!" If men could only develop into better psychologists and more attentive husbands, they would not have to pay so many medical bills.

Of course, more is involved here than just to raise the head slightly from the newspaper and to listen with patent reluctance to whatever gossip and small nothings the woman may have to offer. No, it is necessary to pay real attention, to make it very clear to her that her problems of household or child rearing, her troubles with maids and neighbors are important matters in a homemaker's world since they involve the order and peace of her domain.

But the more deeply marriage partners are able to fathom their differences the better they will be able to understand that they are dealing with fundamental attitudes that cannot be given up or even materially changed. The sooner, too, will they be able to understand that their divergent attitudes rest upon a foundation conditioned by nature itself. Thus they will not be as likely to suspect each other of ill will, obtuseness, or bad manners, but will come to regard and to accept each other's differences as given by nature. In this way, the basic difference between husband and wife loses much of its conflict-potential. It can now be accepted much like a natural phenomenon which may not be pleasant, which cannot be changed either by scolding or by taking offense.

Are we not used to taking rain in our stride as something we cannot change? When it rains we try to adapt ourselves to it. This is precisely the process of transformation which the partners in marriage must attempt with respect to their respective differences. By this process, much severe conflict can be prevented in the marriage. Just as we may be able to find beauty in the rain and to enjoy it, even so the different nature of a husband or wife may suddenly appear in a new light as a result of such a neutral and objective attitude. No longer will the difference irritate us; rather, we will find it delightful!

TELL HER SO

Amid the cares of married life,
In spite of toil and business strife,
If you value your sweet wife,
   Tell her so!

There was a time you thought it bliss
To get the favor of a kiss;
A dozen now won't come amiss —
   Tell her so!

Don't act as if she's passed her prime,
As though to please her were a crime —
If e'er you loved her, now's the time;
   Tell her so!

You are hers and hers alone;
Well you know she's all your own;
Don't wait to carve it on the stone —
   Tell her so!

Never let her heart grow cold;
Richer beauties will unfold.
She is worth her weight in gold;
   Tell her so!

—AUTHOR UNKNOWN

Rx FOR MARITAL ILLNESS

by A. Dudley Dennison, M.D.

Chief of Cardiology, Veterans Hospital, Des Moines, Iowa

The old ship of matrimony that God launched in the Garden of Eden has been caught in a cyclone of change. Of every dozen wedded couples (according to studies by John Cuber and Peggy Harroff), four will jump overboard, six will stay lashed on deck because of utilitarian interests — children, career, family, church, etc. — without joy or love, and only two will enjoy what Dr. Joyce Brothers calls "total" marriages, where they will share a lifetime of happiness. A Gallup poll found three of four women arguing that if they could turn back the calendar they would not pick the same husband.

In his *Habitation of Dragons* Keith Miller tells about conducting a conference for the deacons of a large church. When two "witnesses" he'd brought along began to talk about the temptations of extramarital sex, the pastor got uptight and told Keith, "Our men are dedicated Christians; I know them personally. You'll offend them."

Miller retired to his room to ponder how the conference might better minister to the dedicated deacons. A knock came at the door. It was one of the deacons who wanted to confess and pray. Four more "dedicated" deacons came to him that night, all confessing problems with extramarital sex.

Some very loud voices are shouting that wedlock is a padlock which leads to deadlock, and that the first institution God established has outlived its usefulness.

On the assumption that it isn't the institution that's sick but the personnel, I'm going to try and diagnose the major causes of marital illness. The emphasis on self-fulfillment and self-identity is at the top of my chart. This came in part as a reaction to the shrinkage of personal identity in modern society. Young people particularly rebel and refuse to be baked in the ovens of conformity. With their new music and strange dress, they cry: "Do not fold, staple, or mutilate. I want to be free, to be me."

Women's Lib has applied the goals of the youth revolution to the "better half" of the human race. As a typical male chauvinist, I've made the typical jokes about the screaming bra-burners in the movement. As I was telling a friend the other day, "They're the nicest bunch of fellas you'd ever want to meet."

Then I come down off my royal throne and recognize that the "libbers" have some legitimate gripes. They're not all out to take the gender from rest-room doors. Women should rebel against being regarded as parasites, slaves, and objects. They should have equal opportunity in employment and society. However, there are some things only men can do, just as there are some things only women can do.

As one who has observed the interpersonal relationships of men and women from a medical viewpoint, I seriously question whether the anti-biblical, pseudo-emancipation of women called for by the Lib leaders will bring women happiness.

The self-fulfillment cult has captured a lot of men also, who are sort of astronauts in reverse. Each thinks the world revolves around himself. A "reverse astronaut" looks for a mate that excites his sex glands and swells his ego. He shows off his wife like a new car. When her paint job fades and her engine loses its get up and go, he's ready to trade her in for a new model.

Another self-fulfillment type marries a girl he thinks will speed him on the road to success. When she doesn't turn him into an instant wonder, he turns to another woman more promising.

A second cause for marriage malaise in these times is the overemphasis on sex. Sex is promoted as physical enjoyment totally apart from love and the sanctity of marriage as so clearly described in Scripture. Young people read the literature written by sex experts (some of whom have notoriously unhappy marriages themselves) and get grandiose ideas of what the relationship should be. They sleep around to get experience or sleep with their fiancés. The wedding night proves unexciting; they've opened their presents before Christmas and find themselves bored by the celebration.

Much misery is propounded by striving for Olympic performance in bed. One or the other becomes disappointed at not reaching the peak of ecstasy described in a sex manual. Actually, good sex adjustment is a goal to be attained and half the fun is getting there.

The pace of modern life is a third factor in problem marriages. Husband is gone from six to six and arrives home with bulging briefcase after a hard day of committee meetings, anxious to get some work done. Wife has a mothers' meeting at the school or a missionary council at the church. Son has Boy Scouts and after that a swim meet. Sister is rehearsing for a play at church. The home is only a crossroads service station where they meet for refueling. The result is a fragmented marriage and divided home with few common interests.

Some husbands use busyness as an excuse to avoid closeness and intimacy in marriage. They may purposely, but unconsciously, give much time to others — business associate, golfing partner — in order to have little time for their mates. They are rarely in the mood to make love and seldom say or do anything endearing or sentimental to the partner.

The suffering half of this marriage may seek emotional satisfactions in a lover. A husband or wife seldom breaks the marriage vows on the spur of a momentary temptation. Unfaithfulness is usually the last straw in a strained, armslength relationship.

A fourth disturber of marital harmony is the spirit of materialism. I have known many businessmen who are sacrificing marital happiness upon the altar of success. They work long hours and take long business trips to keep climbing the corporate ladder, only to find that when they reach the top their marriage has crashed on the rocks below.

Financial difficulty is frequently rated at the top of the problems which make marriage hard. But fiscal conflicts are usually symptoms, not causes. A husband gets even with his frigid wife by withholding money. Or a wife takes revenge on her husband's indifference by going on a charging spree. Is money at fault? No. One or both are undisciplined, irresponsible, and selfish.

Communication block is another sign that a marriage is in trouble. A communication channel usually doesn't get blocked by one abrasive landslide of conflict. The blockage builds up like river silt, a little at a time and so slowly it's hardly noticed. The couple drifts apart gradually, each opening new channels outside the home, until finally they are like two strangers sharing a table in a crowded restaurant.

The little courtesies and sentiments of courtship fade with the wedding bouquet. Flowers and candy and special kisses vanish in the hurry and scurry of life. Each takes the other for granted. The glue of romantic love starts to crack. Little irritations and resentments begin smoldering beneath the surface. He begins embracing her like he's in a football game and will get penalized for holding. The marriage is in trouble.

Regarding remedies for the miseries of marital diseases:

First of all, accept your mate for what she is. This is why it's good to know your intended well before taking the final leap. Puppy love with a short leash on courtship can lead to a dog's life. But whether you had a long or a short engagement, the success of your marriage may hinge upon acceptance of your partner's total person. If you truly love your mate, you will continue to be blind to her many faults. Love can be delightfully blind, even after marriage.

Don't take your wife for granted. Remember birthdays and anniversaries and be not like the fellow who went with his wife to a psychiatrist and said, "Old what's-her-name here says I'm forgetful." Surprise her with flowers and candy and moonlight drives in the country. She'll meet you at the door with her hair combed, a smile, and a contraction of the lips which results from an expansion of the heart.

Be careful not to dump all the troubles of a rough day into your wife's lap in one grumpy moment. Find a relaxed moment, perhaps after the children are in bed, to tell her about disappointments and difficulties. And she will lovingly reciprocate by listening to and sympathizing with your tale of woe.

Reserve time for aloneness and allow neither children, in-laws, neighbors, church activities, pesky salesmen, or work brought home from the office to interfere. Take occasional honeymoons, be they only for a night, just to get away.

Make sex loving and exciting. Do not make love just for the sake of loving, but for the response of your lover. Remember: "The wife hath not power of her own body, but the husband; and likewise also the husband hath not power of his own body, but the wife" (1 Corinthians 7:4).

Develop the art of admitting your faults and proving your repentance by changing your ways. An honest "I'm sorry" is soothing the first time and perhaps even the second and third time, but unless you put your money where your mouth is your confession will be sand in her craw.

You must not throw a lighted match into the spilled gasoline of a tense situation, remembering that "a soft answer turneth away wrath; but grievous words stir up anger" (Proverbs 15:1).

Always speak in the plural regarding joint interests. Not "my home" but "our home." Not "my career" but "our career." Not "my baby" but "our baby." Not "my vacation" but "our vacation."

Say with Joshua, "As for me and my house, we will serve the Lord" (Joshua 24:15). Always worship together and serve together in the same church, and pray together at home.

For six months I lived in a Des Moines motel room without my wife. Ginny had to stay behind in Tennessee and sell our house and wait until our daughter finished her senior year of high school. The separation was painful but it helped us consolidate more richly our thoughts about one another.

Two incidents stand out during that marital hiatus. One involved a mild degree of tension during a telephone talk regarding furniture. Several days later a letter arrived with a caricature of an ugly female under a horrible hairdo and the words: "It means a lot to have someone like you." Inside I read, "A lot of time, a lot of frustration, a lot of headaches, a lot of worry — but a lot of fun." In the same mail was a cassette Ginny had recorded for me.

I slipped it into my recorder and there were the old songs we loved, words of loneliness, words of affection, words of commitment in love. Sitting alone in the motel room, tears began washing my cheeks. The phone rang and I answered it as if I had cotton in my nose. It was Ginny alerting me to the possibility of the sale of our house. Certainly we had bombarded heaven for this event to take place. "Do you have a cold? You sound terrible. What's the matter?" she asked. I had to confess that her recording had broken me up. So the lady Eve knew that the man Adam loved her. Man — the left ventricle of the marital heart — was still attached to his woman, the right ventricle. We were miles apart, but together in heart.

There is no greater earthly relationship.

GOLDEN SILENCE

It is a false notion that every happy marriage needs a few good knockdown and dragout squabbles. The sweetness of making up can never pay for the damage which is done, because a word is more than a word. A word is a deed. Once spoken, it stamps itself upon the mind of the person by whom it is spoken, and it sets up a barrier against the person to whom it is spoken. "Be ye angry," says Paul, "and sin not." It may not be possible not to be angry, but patience makes it possible not to allow anger to express itself. There is many a home intact today because some things which were felt were never spoken.

—JOHN C. WYNN

MAKE HER HAPPY

by Cecil G. Osborne

Regional Director, Yokefellows, Inc.

There are many reasons for the breakup of marriages, but the most common one is never mentioned in divorce complaints: each of the marriage partners is waiting for the other to meet his needs.

Selfishness cries, "Meet my needs! Love me! Love me even when I am unlovable, hysterical, or uncommunicative, or impossible." Love says, "Let me try to meet your needs. Tell me what it is that you want or need, and I will do my best to comply. If I cannot do so at the moment, I will explain why, as patiently as I can; but I will try to meet your needs to the best of my ability."

There are two basic needs which every individual possesses: to love and be loved; and to feel worthwhile. Anything we can do to meet these basic needs is an act of love. Failure to meet them results in heartache, disillusionment, despair, and often divorce. From years of counseling, let me make a few suggestions.

Treat your wife with strength and gentleness. No matter how self-reliant a woman may be; regardless of her intelligence, capability, and drive; even if she seems dominant there is something within her which wants to "lean" on a man. She would like to be swept off her feet, and then taken care of with gentleness and strength. This combination of strength and tenderness is not easily achieved if one does not possess it innately, but you can work at it. You may make mistakes, but with patience and determination you can satisfy your wife's inner need for emotional security with a quiet strength that is gentle and tender.

Give ample praise and reassurance. The role of mother renders the woman much more vulnerable and insecure. Instinctively she feels a need for someone to protect her and her children and to provide for the family. This generates a kind of all-pervasive insecurity which exists whether there are children or not, or after the children have left the nest. Because of this and other factors, women need considerable reassurance. It can be given in the form of praise, recognition, commendation, or simply by saying often: "I love you!" When a woman asks, "Do you love me?" she isn't asking for information. She is asking for reassurance.

Define the areas of responsibility. If two men are in partnership, they must work out the spheres of activity and have them clearly defined. The same thing holds with equal force in a marriage relationship.

Some areas seem clearly enough defined. Your wife takes care of the house, she cooks, and she has the primary responsibility for the children, particularly when they are very young. You earn the living. But there are many other less clearly defined areas.

Who is responsible for the lawn, choosing the new car, deciding where to spend the vacation? Who has the veto power on making investments or where to live? Who decides when to buy a new washing machine or new furniture? Who casts the deciding vote concerning what to do on weekends?

You, as husband, could easily abdicate responsibility by saying, "Look, dear, you're a lot better at that than I am. Why don't you just take care of it and not bother me with details?"

There is, to the male, a "peculiarity" of the feminine nature which — in most cases — wants the husband to participate. A wife often feels more "secure" if she can talk things over with her husband. She may choose a time to do this when you want to read, golf, or watch television. You can become grossly irritated over what may seem to you to be minor issues. But life consists not only of major decisions. Marriage is mostly "little things," which to a male can be an excruciating bore. But this is a part of marriage and of living.

A couple must find out for themselves where the various

"spheres of influence" lie: who pays the bills, who casts the deciding vote on buying what house, renting which apartment, where to vacation. A selfish husband or wife may insist on rendering a final verdict on all decisions, major and minor; but marriage involves resolving the incompatible needs of two different people.

Avoid criticism. A man who constantly criticizes and condemns his wife can produce numerous negative results in his wife. She may become deeply depressed through repressing her hostility; develop one or more physical symptoms, since the mind tends to hand its pain over to the body; become hostile, emotionally unresponsive, or sexually frigid; lose her identity through being constantly beaten down; unload her resentment onto the children and cause emotional disturbances in them; decide to give up the marriage.

A regular barrage of criticism, even when warranted, is always destructive. In fact, almost all criticism is destructive. There is usually a better way to achieve results. Just because we are married, we do not have the right to be insulting or tactless and critical. The marriage license is not a license to insult.

Remember the importance of "little things." Men are usually less sentimental than women and attach less importance to such things as birthdays, anniversaries, and "little" gestures which mean much to women. Love is not just a feeling; it involves positive actions which can mean a great deal to a woman.

Men are nearly always surprised to discover how much "little things" (as they deem them to be) mean to a woman — an unexpected gift, a compliment on a new dress, or a sincere, "You look great with the new hairdo, Honey."

"I don't want to have to remind my husband of our anniversaries," one wife said. "That takes all the fun out of it; and I don't want to have to make all the suggestions about going out, or to dinner. I'd love it if just once he'd initiate something, take the lead, show me that he cares, plan something for us without asking me." This is a legitimate female need, and a husband must recognize it if he is to be an adequate marriage partner.

Recognize her need for togetherness. No two women are identical in their needs, of course, but in general women tend more often than men to require a sense of "togetherness." A wife may often want more of her husband's time and attention than he feels like giving her. Togetherness does not imply that we will go through life hand in hand, always enjoying identical things to the same degree. We are still individual humans with divergent needs and tastes. We must respect the needs of others and compromise cheerfully when necessary. Only the immature and childish demand to have their way under all circumstances.

Give her a sense of security. A woman's need for security is much greater than most men imagine. It can be provided by a husband who is strong, gentle, and considerate. But in specific areas women's needs vary. Many women derive a sense of security from having a husband who does household repairs. This means he is interested in the nest and thus interested in her. Any man can mow a lawn, which is also related to nest-building, or rake leaves, or help move the furniture (if she is a "furniture mover"), or at least take an interest in her daily activities.

If your wife derives a sense of security from having a bank account of her own, or her own savings account, go along with it. It may not make sense to you, but this is not as important as her sense of security. It need not be logical. Don't try to run your marriage on a steady diet of logic; feelings are just as important as logic, often more so.

Recognize the validity of her moods. Women tend to have somewhat stronger mood variations than most men. Part of this can be attributed to the monthly cycle. With this a husband must learn to be patient and considerate. A woman can appear to be illogical and utterly irrational at times, at least to the male mind which wants things tidy and logical. You may as well accept her variations in mood as inevitable. Don't be panicked or disturbed by mood swings. Ride them out with patience and kindly indulgence. Don't take it personally or tell her to "snap out of it."

Cooperate with her in every effort to improve your marriage. Women are insatiable, and men are obtuse. They can be insatiable in their desire to make a better marriage. Your wife may want to read a book on marriage or communication or child rearing. Your male ego, if it is a bit weak, may reject this suggested reading, believing there is an implied criticism in her handing you the book to read.

Read it! What do you have to lose? You may even learn something. Any husband could read a dozen or two books on marriage and profit from the experience.

If she encourages you to visit a marriage counselor with her, or join a group, or go to a series of lectures on marriage or child rearing, by all means go. Go along with her graciously and good-naturedly. A marriage counselor can cost a great deal less than a divorce and years and years of child support, besides saving a marriage and avoiding the tears and pain of divorce.

Discover her particular, individual needs and try to meet them. No two wives are alike. The one you married is different from any other woman. She has her own particular set of likes and dislikes, moods, and emotional needs. Her needs may seem limitless at first, or unreasonable. Perhaps you cannot meet all of her needs at once. But you can try to discover what she needs, wants, appreciates; you can seek to meet those needs within your capacity. This does not mean catering to childish whims, but it can mean going along with something that may seem illogical or unimportant to you. If it makes her happy and gives her a sense of satisfaction, try to satisfy the need.

Every man who is happy at home is a successful man, even if he has failed in everything else.

—WILLIAM LYON PHELPS

WHEN THE WINE RUNS OUT

by G. R. Slater

Minister, St. Matthew's United Church, Toronto, Canada

Remember the Bible story of the wedding at Cana, when the supply of wine ran out?

In a sense, the "wine" of marriage always runs out, and there are days of emptiness when the early wine of rapture runs dry, and the promise of a paradise of love fails. But the point which saves the story, and gives us hope, is that Jesus was there to supply what was lacking. The good news is that when Christ comes into marriage and family life, he replenishes what has been used up and exhausted. There is a new quality, a "royal wine" which he makes to flow freely for us.

Alongside this story let us put the portrait of love which Paul draws in 1 Corinthians 13: "Love is patient and kind; love is not jealous or boastful; it is not arrogant or rude. Love does not insist on its own way; it is not irritable or resentful; it does not rejoice at wrong, but rejoices in the right. Love bears all things, believes all things, hopes all things, endures all things. Love never ends." The "royal wine" by which Christ replenishes and fulfills a marriage is none other than this kind of love. When such love enters a marriage, it brings a new spirit, and several things happen.

1. It fosters unselfishness. We have only to look around us to see the pressures which oppose any such altruistic and loving attitude. Exploitation can be found in virtually every sphere of modern life, and in recent years it has laid rude hands upon the highest and greatest gift of all — human personality. Sales people, teachers, executives, and television and radio figures are selling personality as their basic commodity. Erich Fromm has noted that we are a society of consumption: like a great mouth we devour experience and substance. The danger is that we will consume the talents and personalities of people. Now, says Fromm, we have arrived at the point where "sex has become one of the main objects of consumption."

All of this has implications for marriage, for the kind of love which Christ brings is totally opposite to exploitation. It is self-forgetful, self-giving. It cares for the other person as an individual. Martin Luther said that man is the one being who is "all curled up in himself." The love which Christ inspires draws man out of himself, uncurls him so that he can reach out and genuinely embrace another human being. When this love possesses us, we come to know the other person not just as a means to our own happiness and security, but as a child of God.

2. *It also fosters realism.* This is love with its eyes wide open. Therefore it recognizes that no marriage is perfect — which is no news to married people. Realism demands that we recognize the difficulties of marriage; love says we can still have unity through difficulties.

We are seeking too much from marriage today. Life has become impersonal. Our circle of friends changes often, and there are few long-time friendships. The family has cut itself adrift from formerly close kinship bonds. Now all the closeness and intimacy previously shared in these other ways among many people is being focused on one person, and the whole load is placed on one pair of shoulders — the husband's or the wife's. It is only realistic to recognize the strain that this excessive closeness and extreme demand places upon both husband and wife. One cannot be expected to be mate, brother, father, friend, and psychiatrist all rolled up in one.

Obviously, there is going to be tension. When anyone who has been married for many years tells me he has never had an argument with his spouse, I feel like asking, "What's wrong? Don't you care enough to differ? Has communication broken down to that degree? Or is one of you a 'yes-man'?"

Conflict can be creative, and the love which is "patient

and kind" is able to embrace tensions creatively in at least two ways:

First, it makes possible an openness and honesty about one's disappointments. Often a person feels that his faith forbids him to be honest or critical with his mate, but you owe it to your marriage partner to let her know how you feel. Such openness can be the basis of a new beginning and partnership at a deeper level.

The love that "bears all things" is necessary to accept the truth about yourself. Realism demands that you express these feelings within the setting of love and acceptance, for otherwise they will come out elsewhere, and hostility will be vented on the children or on fellow workers.

What is more, the feelings of self-abnegation which prompt a person to suffer in silence rather than risk a confrontation may in fact be destructive. "Love your neighbor as yourself" implies, beyond the obvious, that we are to respect our own rights and feelings.

Second, this love that is at liberty to be realistic calls us to recognize that marriage is something that must be worked out. It is not like a coat that is put on, but like a flower that grows. As one elderly lady testified, "Love is what you go through together." It is the recognition, therefore, that you have some needs which are not going to be met by the other person, and that there are some things upon which you will never totally agree. Realism demands patience and a willingness to adjust. The art of marriage, it has been said, is in maintaining equilibrium through the various changes and adjustments of life together.

3. *The love which Christ brings into marriage requires a sense of responsibility.* Marriage obligates two people to each other in a final and complete sense. When two young people come to the altar, the minister does not ask them, "Are you in love?" but "Wilt thou love . . . ?" It is not a declaration of how you feel about someone, but a pledge of your fidelity and lifelong loyalty to that person.

It also means responsibility to others. One reason so many marriages founder and fail is that we have not stressed the obligation that married people have to society. Marriage can never be merely the isolated experience of two people. Like the stone thrown into a pond, its repercussions can be felt on the farthest shore, for good or bad. The same thing holds true of premarital relations.

4. *Finally, the presence of Christ gives a grace to marriage.* By that I mean a plus, a blessing, and a power beyond the ordinary. It is significant that the marriage of man and woman is the favorite image which the Bible uses for God's relationship to his people. And Jesus spoke of himself as the bridegroom and believers as his bride. There is something wonderful about a human relationship which partakes of divine overtones like that.

There is something divine in true marriage. It is like a triangle: it takes three to get married — a man, a woman, and God. Francis de Sales put it this way, "If the glue is good, two pieces of wood glued together will cleave so fast to each other that they can be more easily broken in any other place than where they were joined. God glues the husband to the wife with his own blood."

This means that every marriage needs the miracle of God's presence. It needs to invite him in so that he can introduce his reconciling grace into the material of two lives. That grace is not a buttress thrown up from the outside to hold up the walls of marriage when they are unable to stand by themselves. It is the "glue" which provides the conditions of personal responsibility, patience, and understanding by which two persons adhere to each other in willing faithfulness.

3

The Man and His Children

LIKE FATHER, LIKE SON

by Leslie Flynn

Minister, Grace Conservative Baptist Church, Nanuet, N.Y.

A father heard a roar of laughter from the other members of the family and he walked into the hallway in time to see his little boy coming down the stairs dressed in a full suit of Dad's clothing. He had tied a string around the bottoms of the trousers and pulled the waistband up under his arms. The long coat dragged on the floor. The big hat flopped to his ears. His feet were lost in his father's size-eleven shoes which clomped down the steps. After joining in the laughter, the father said, "I'm going to take a picture. There's real truth here. My little boy wants to be like his father." He snapped the camera, later putting the developed picture in his desk. Every time he opened the drawer the father saw the snapshot which seemed to say, "Look, Daddy, I'm following you. I want to be like you!"

One child, asked on a questionnaire if he were a Christian, wrote, "I am not a Christian because my father is not a Christian, and I am the same thing."

Need for Interest

One policeman said, "From the amount of vandalism that goes on, you'd think that kids have no parents." A police reporter related, "At 4 A.M. an unhappy father arrived at the police station to complain about his car being held as evidence. 'Your *car!*' shouted a weary detective. 'Aren't you concerned about your son?' The father shrugged his shoulders. His parting remark was a corker, 'Make sure the windows of my car are closed, in case it rains!' "

One Christian worker testifies, "The biggest influence in my life was my father. He spent a great deal of time teaching me how to be a person. As I grew up, he made it a policy every evening to spend an hour with my brother and myself, teaching us something, perhaps reading us something from the newspaper and then explaining it. This hour after supper lasted till I was married at eighteen. This is all the more remarkable since my father had only an eighth-grade education."

EFFECT OF ATMOSPHERE

Finding their way to a particular profession is not accidental for many successful men. Mickey Mantle, former home-run slugger for the New York Yankees, was deeply influenced by his father. Mantle wrote, "According to Mother I was still in the cradle when Dad asked her to make a baseball hat for me. When I was five he had her cut down his baseball trousers and sew together my first uniform. Also when I was five, he began teaching me how to switch-hit; that is, to hit left-handed against right-hand pitchers, and right-handed against left-hand pitchers, which gives a hitter a big advantage. Dad was a left-hander, Grandpa a right-hander. Every day after work they'd start a five-hour batting session. Both would toss tennis balls at me in our front yard as hard as they could. I'd bat right-handed against Dad, and switch to left-handed against Grandpa. When I hit the ball hard over the house or through somebody's window they would count it a run. I'm probably the only kid around who made his old man proud of him by breaking windows. Dad hammered baseball into me for recreation. But he did more than that. He taught me confidence. Dad was thirty-five and I was fifteen when he let me play with him on the local baseball team."

Abraham's nephew, Lot, paid an exorbitant price for his selfish choice of land near Sodom, a city whose very name has come to refer to a vice. His family imbibed such a deep attraction for this city of exceeding wickedness that his wife lost her life at the hour of its destruction. Unlike Lot, many modern men have selected the site of new homes because of proximity to a Bible-preaching church where their children would receive Christian instruction and fellowship.

IMPORTANCE OF INSTRUCTION

Walter Reuther, the late UAW labor leader, said his pattern of life was molded by his father who was a union organizer. Reuther's father conducted debates at home on issues like capital punishment and the right to strike. Said the father: "It was no accident that three of my sons became labor officials." Nor is it any accident that Walter Reuther could more than hold his own in a debate.

Fathers in Israel were charged to teach God's law diligently to their children, both formally and informally. Today many fathers would choke if they tried to talk of God to their children. Author Will Durant tells of a little girl who came to her mother with the age-old question, "Mother, what is God like?" Mother hesitated, then said, "You'd better ask Daddy." She did. He too hesitated. Later in her childish possessions was found a slip of paper with this free verse:

I asked my mother what God was like.
She did not know.
Then I asked my father, who knows more than anyone
    else in the world, what God was like.
He did not know.
I think if I had lived as long as my mother or my father
I would know something about God.

Theodore Epp, Back to the Bible program broadcaster, says, "The one man who had the greatest effect on my life was my father. He taught me the necessity of absolute dependence on Christ for a useful Christian life." George

Beverly Shea, soloist for the Billy Graham crusades, credits the spiritual counseling of his father as the greatest single influence on his life.

EXERCISE OF DISCIPLINE

The Bible repeatedly stresses the need for fatherly discipline. "Withhold not correction from the child: for if thou beatest him with the rod, he shall not die. Thou shalt beat him with the rod, and shalt deliver his soul from hell" (Proverbs 23:13, 14).

Someone said, "Everything in the modern home is run by a switch except the children." Of course, overstrictness is as wrong as overindulgence, but discipline is a major need of every child. Fathers who let their offspring have their own way are paving the route for later rebellion against constituted authority, which is the essence of delinquency. A little boy refused to close a door that his father asked him to shut. A little girl who overheard was asked later what the little boy needed. Instead of: "A whipping," she answered, "A father."

POWER OF EXAMPLE

One young man said to his father, "When I was young, there were times when you set out to tell me how to live the good life. I could always tell such moments and closed my ears and my mind. Your most influential moments were your most inadvertent ones. I imitated what you really were, not what you said." Children react much less to what grown-ups say than to the intangibles in the home. Someone said, "Till a boy is fifteen he does what his father says; after that he does what his father does."

The New York Times carried an article which gave the findings of a psychiatrist after a four-year study of Long Island delinquents. It carried the heading: "Delinquent Boys From Well-To-Do-Homes Say Fathers Set Double Standards." The conclusion of the article was this: "The affluent teen-age boy who steals hub caps, crashes house parties, and drinks too much is very likely to have learned delinquency at his father's knee." Though these fathers tried to impress on their sons the necessity for diligence, perseverance, and respect for the Golden Rule, at the same time they boasted of shady business conquests or of truancy in boyhood or of taking the shortcut to success. The conflict between precept and example greatly confused the boys, according to the psychiatrist. He added that even if the boys sensed their father's behavior was reprehensible they could hardly reject his example.

One psychologist suggested that a father can better understand his teen-age boy or girl if he asks himself, "What is there about me which my child is copying?"

A man who had violated a minor traffic law was given a ticket by a police officer. His son was with him. The father fumed all the way home, vowing he would get the matter fixed by friends at the city hall, and that he would give the officer a hard time because of it. Cooling off, he began to realize what his performance was teaching his son. Next day he explained to his boy how a person says things in anger that he doesn't really mean. Then he took his son with him to court, pleaded guilty, and paid the fine. On the way home he talked with the boy about the relation of traffic laws to safety. That lad will have a healthier respect for policemen and law because of a wise father's good example.

One Saturday night a car careened off a highway, killing the young man driving and seriously injuring his companion, a seventeen-year-old girl, who was very popular in high school. The girl's mother had been uneasy all evening for she thought she had seen a bottle in the young man's pocket as the couple left the home. Reaching the hospital, the girl's parents learned that the couple had been drinking. The bottle had been found in the car. The father left the hospital in a rage, muttering, "If I could find the person that sold my daughter that whiskey, I'd — I'd kill him!" Returning home, he headed for his liquor cabinet to get something to quiet his nerves. There on the shelf inside the cabinet was a note in his daughter's handwriting, "Dear Dad, we hope you won't mind us taking your whiskey tonight."

The most important example of all is for a father to accept Christ as his personal Savior, confess him before others, then live a dedicated life for Christ. A father once took his little boy on his lap and described what a Christian was. When he was through, the little boy asked a question that pierced his father's heart: "Daddy, have I ever seen one?"

In early life I had nearly been betrayed into the principles of spiritual infidelity, but there was one argument in favor of Christianity that I could not refute, and that was the consistent character and example of my own father.

—QUARLES

FATHERS OF ORPHANS

by Joel Nederhood

Radio Speaker, Back to God Hour

A research team investigating juvenile delinquency in a New York City slum was astonished to find a world without fathers. After studying the children and talking with their mothers, they turned to examine the fathers. But they were nowhere to be found. A *New York Times Magazine* article reported, "The Youth Board realized it had penetrated into a world where there is no father. The welfare world of New York is a fatherless world. The father is an impregnator. He vanishes after he has planted his seed. He is frightened by the bloom."

You do not have to go to the slum areas of large cities, however, to find fathers who are afraid of their offspring and who try to abandon them. Many fathers who support their children very well actually desert them. Max Lerner, a careful observer of modern life, writes of "vanishing fathers." In a magazine article he stated: "The vanishing father is perhaps the central fact of the changing American family structure today." Prof. Lerner was not talking about the welfare world of large cities; he was talking about modern family life in general.

Modern fathers abandon their children in a variety of ways. First of all, some do literally desert their wives and children. They disappear and their families never receive one cent from them. This occurs frequently in slum areas, though not exclusively, by any means. Second, many men practically desert their families by staying away from home a great deal. They support their families, but their children seldom see them. The pressure of business and professional life is so great they never leave their work long enough to pay sustained attention to their children.

But most men abandon their children in a very ordinary way: they support their families well and they are home enough, but they fail to be real fathers. They play with their children occasionally, but they have nothing in common with them. They seem withdrawn and preoccupied. They sit for hours with magazines or newspapers or in front of their television sets, and they let their children know that they do not appreciate being bothered. Perhaps they have a hobby: they work hours making things out of wood or metal, but they are not interested in molding their children's lives. As the years go on, the children grow further away from their father.

No matter how a father chooses to abandon his children, the results are always the same. As long as he refuses to face his deepest responsibilities as a father, his children are orphans for all practical purposes. If a father only provides his children with physical necessities, he provides them with no more than children receive who have been institutionalized because they have no parents. If a father refuses to discharge the most important responsibilities of fatherhood, he cannot expect his wife to be a real mother either. Without the assistance of her husband, a mother is bound to become discouraged.

Mothers who receive no help from their husbands often try to escape the home themselves by finding work. In this way their insecurity and the insecurity of their children can be partially met by a few material goods they could not have otherwise. In such situations, the children drift aimlessly, with some guidance from their teachers and constant pressures from their friends. They receive nothing but clothing, food, and shelter from their parents. But they need so much more than that. They are homeless children, orphaned by a father who is not man enough to be a real father and by a mother whose husband never helps her be what a mother should be.

Some analysts of the modern family explain the abandonment this way: When men are at home they want to relax; they have problems enough at work; when they are "off the clock," they do not want to be bothered with important decisions; when trouble develops in their families, they prefer to look the other way; they fail to take their children seriously and fail to discipline them.

These are good explanations, but they don't go to the root of the problem. The question still remains: "Where did men ever get the idea that the home is a recreation center?" According to the Bible, the home is the heart of human society, the most important place we spend our time. When it comes right down to it, the real reason fathers abandon their families is that they are either ignorant of the biblical description of the grand task of a father, or they reject it. Many modern fathers have lost sight of God and knowledge of his holy Word. That is the basic reason they are fathers of orphans.

In the Bible, beginning in the Old Testament, the father is the individual charged with the great task of transmitting true faith in the living God from his generation to the next. In Psalm 78 the father's story of God's judgment and salvation is told in epic language. In verses 5, 6, and 7 of that Psalm we read: "He . . . appointed a law in Israel, which he commanded our fathers, that they should make them known to their children: that the generations to come might know them, even the children which should be born; who should arise and declare them to their children that they might set their hope in God, and not forget the works of God but keep his commandments." In many instances in the Old Testament, the father pronounced God's blessing over the heads of his children.

The same high description of a father's responsibility is found in the New Testament. In Ephesians 5 his role in the family is compared to Christ's "role" in the Church. "The husband is the head of the wife, even as Christ is the head of the Church." Ephesians 6:4 describes his task this way: "And, ye fathers, provoke not your children to wrath, but bring them up in the nurture and admonition of the Lord." This means that the primary responsibility for the spiritual nurture of the children belongs to the father. In discharging this responsibility he is dependent upon his wife. As the mother spends the most time with the children, she will do much of the teaching. But the father is responsible for his wife's spiritual welfare and for their children's.

By means of the family God is pleased to communicate the Christian message from one generation to another. Within the family, the father is called to a high and noble service. When the family disintegrates or fails to be what it should be, the father is responsible for its collapse.

We can understand the noble dimensions of true fatherhood only if we think of the father's task as similar to the work of Christ in the Church. Christ's relation to his Church can be described this way: he is the church's chief prophet, its only high priest, and its eternal King. The father, who is called to be Christ's representative within the family, must be in a sense the prophet, priest, and king for his family.

When a father acts as a prophet within his family, he carefully provides for the spiritual nurture of his wife and children. He leads his family in the study of the Word of God. Many fathers make sure that the Bible is read when the family is together at meal time. As a prophet, the father must also make sure that the activities of the home do not interfere with regular church attendance and with useful observance of the Lord's day. He chooses a church for his family in which the Word of God is faithfully proclaimed.

As the representative of Christ, the father is also called to be a priest in his home. Christ's priestly work consists of his sacrifice on the cross and his prayers on behalf of his people. A father too must be willing to sacrifice for the spiritual welfare of his children. If his job is detrimental to his family's spiritual welfare, he must find another. As priest, the father also leads the family in prayer. Most fathers who take this seriously make sure that prayer is always offered when the family is gathered together for their meals.

As priest of his family, the father also calls his family together in times of crisis and tension for special prayer. And as priest a Christian father continually prays for his wife and children.

Finally, as Christ's representative, the father also exercises the office of king. Christ is the King of his Church and he exercises his authority by making his will known through his Word and his Spirit. As king within the home, the father is not to be a tyrant, but, following Christ's example, he uses the Word of God to make God's will known to his wife and children. The father must be the seat of authority within the family structure.

He rules his family, first of all, by exhibiting proper conduct in his own life. Since his own life has been formed by the testimony of the Scriptures, he displays to his family what it means to be a Christian. He also rules by demanding certain activity from his children and prohibiting other conduct. When his children turn to him for guidance they feel at once that his counsel has been drawn from the Bible itself, even though their father does not unctuously quote texts to them. They know him as a man of God and thus they are confident that his guidance is exceptionally useful. This is the grand and noble calling of fatherhood.

Look at your children. If all you are giving them is food, clothing, and shelter, you are giving them no more than animals give their young: your children are really orphans after all. You can be a real father to your children, and God may use you to give them their most precious possession — their faith in the Lord Jesus Christ.

HELP YOUR SON BECOME A MAN

by Annetta H. Bridges

Author and Educator

Harry, with top credentials and education, can never hold onto a job.

Bill was a capable swimmer, but when it was time to rescue a pal, he didn't dive in.

Tom seemed like a reasonable husband — but was insanely jealous of his new baby.

Sam handled high school well, it appeared — but college cracked him up.

And thousands of demonstrators, fervent in their "beliefs," have copped out of the normal stream of life — not because they don't want the fruits of labor, but because they're scared of the competition or the responsibility.

In his famous prayer, "Build Me a Son, O Lord," General Douglas MacArthur asks for a son who would be strong enough to know when he is weak and brave enough to face himself when he is afraid — one who is proud and unbending in honest defeat, but humble and gentle in victory.

That prayer might have described the sons of yesterday's generation; but today, with few recognizable opportunities for challenges, it's not easy for a boy to become a man. And maybe that's just it: it looks so easy, and it's not.

Growing into a man is never easy, and it's something that must be done alone, part of the time. But that doesn't mean that the men of the world can't point a kid in the right direction. In today's atmosphere of violence, demands, robberies, and copouts, it's not even easy to find somebody worth emulating. But that doesn't mean we can't have boys that can become real men, either. All it takes is somebody willing to do what yesterday's dads did — put the boys with the men a part of the time — until they become men themselves.

Women are necessary, of course — they got us here,

didn't they? But once a boy is a few years old, if he doesn't have a man to admire and imitate and look up to, there are formidable obstacles in his becoming a functioning member of the school called the world.

Today, with Dad in the office or on the road or in the factory, boys honestly often have no idea how their own fathers prove their manhood — or what they do even to put bread on the table.

Time was when a boy proved his manhood in many ways. He worked, if he wanted food to eat and a fire to warm by. He milked the cows, cut the wood, and killed the squirrel or rabbit or deer for supper. The art of getting along was learned through keeping your mouth shut when superiors spoke until you'd learned something worth saying, and through pitting your skills against the elements of nature. To prove he was a man, a boy plowed a straight row, brought home an enemy scalp, or whipped the town bully.

Today, it's different. Today, about all a boy's got for a pattern is a woman who's trying to be both father and mother or a teacher who may have a whole two minutes of undivided attention to give him during the course of listening to 150 other students all day, every day.

It takes men to build men; and though we may provide sports cars and ski equipment and boxing experience and a thousand other things bought with money, neither these nor any other asset in the world will take the place of boys associating with men — genuine men who have proven their manhood and who don't need to go around parading it every day. A real man, boys need to see, doesn't have to bolster his courage with alcohol or to push his wife and children around; he proves his masculinity by being considerate, protective, concerned, and confident — and by demonstrating it.

If this is hitting where it hurts and you've decided about now that you'd better take Junior on that fishing trip, don't expect that to work any miracle. You can't undo the neglect of years in one weekend. Any boy who's grown used to a warm bed and a full stomach and television or movies or

entertainment at all hours isn't necessarily going to be ec-
static over mosquito bites, a wet camp, and cold beans for
breakfast.

But a talk or a trip together can be a beginning. What's
important is that you teach a boy self-respect and confidence,
so that he doesn't feel compelled to draw attention to himself the rest of his life. (Ask any high school teacher; you
wouldn't believe the big babies he has in his classes, whether
they're fourteen or twenty.)

How do you find opportunities for guiding a boy into manhood today? Well, if we'd look around, we could find a lot
more time to share with boys — provided we're willing to
pause a moment to find what's really important in life. And
it's up to parents to teach the joys of personal accomplishment.

Jim, down the street, doesn't live on a farm, but his dad
taught him while he was small how to paint a house, mend a
fence, plant a garden, and catch a fish. Today, he earns
money at all of these jobs, off and on, while staying out of
mischief and becoming a real man in the process.

Tom can't blaze a trail the way his great-grandfather did,
but he has learned how to clean out stables, deliver papers,
open a wax-and-polish service for the neighborhood cars,
and, thanks to his dad's coaching, has taught a lot of other
kids to swim or ride or wash windows.

And if you're saying your sons are too young or too old
for all this stuff — you're dead wrong. A boy is a boy is a
boy — whether he's two or twenty. And the only way he'll
become a man is for somebody to show him the way.

If you're also saying you simply don't have time to super-
vise any of this sort of thing — well, Dad, you're just too
busy. And that goes whether we're talking about your own
sons or somebody else's. Because tomorrow's world, remember, is made from today's youngsters. And it will be no
better than its men.

Boys need challenges — among men. They need jobs and
chores and the chance to prove themselves in adult and important settings. They needn't be led as sheep to the slaugh-

ter in the competition of big business, but they can be exposed gradually to the world of manhood, before they're suddenly turned out into it with a high school or a college diploma.

Boys can learn respect and tenderness for women — wives, mothers, sisters, teachers, or whatever — only by observing men who practice these traits in the home and in every other conceivable situation. And if fathers are careful, they can earn a son's respect more quickly in this way than in any other. For children, we must remember, learn what they live with — no more, no less.

If a father spends an hour in the evening with his son instead of with a client; if he takes, rather than sends, that son to church; if he sets goals and overcomes obstacles *with* his son rather than *for* him, then he's building the foundation for that boy to become a man among other men some day.

No matter what else any man may or may not have attained in this life, if he's helped turn boys into men, he can know that he's not lived in vain.

You don't need to be right all the time. Your child wants a man for a father, not a formula. He wants real parents, real people, capable of making mistakes without moping about it.
                                        —C. D. WILLIAMS

DAD, YOUR DAUGHTER NEEDS YOU

by John E. Crawford

Author and Clinical Psychologist

Carol's father popped into my office one busy morning with an expression on his usually calm face that betrayed his inner feelings of disappointment. Without a word, he showed me the card he had taken from her bedroom door. It was bluntly phrased:

> This is my room. I keep it the way I like it. I don't want anything touched. Thank you for following these rules about my room. Carol

Has something like that happened in your house? Probably it has. So you know from experience that growing girls (even ones who have seemed pretty tame before) can create some touchy "interpersonal problems" around the house. Your own daughter is not likely to be the exception, unless she still is very young. By twelve, practically every girl is quite skittish about whatever she values as *her* special possessions.

She may dash through the upstairs hall stark naked at times, and never give a thought to the situation. The same day she may scream at you if you have to barge in to get something out of the medicine cabinet while she is taking a bath. The same girl, mind you. No wonder some fathers decide that all girls are a little wacky and there is nothing anybody can do about it!

Your own daughter may understand more about the psychology of fathers (and mothers) than time and circumstances have allowed you to learn about her. Many schools have been offering courses which do an excellent job of encouraging youngsters to try to understand how we think and feel. This healthy new insight certainly is all to the good.

Most fathers do understand their youngsters fairly well. Intelligent youngsters — teen-agers, at least — do comprehend their parents' ideas and feelings much better than these same parents and children like to admit at times. If there were fewer "emotional blocks" in the way, most fathers and daughters would get along with fewer spats and arguments.

Every thoughtful father knows that girls, as well as boys, can go terribly far wrong without the right guidance at home. The best counseling services in the finest school facilities have rarely been able to make up for a lack of guidance from a good father and mother who love their children and who tackle the job as a team.

Your daughter wants you to be the chief executive of the household on some matters, with her mother the chief on other matters. She wants you both to be intelligent executives so the household runs as smoothly as it can.

She wants to see in her mother a wise, mature woman who loves you, respects you, and can talk to you about all important issues in the family. She needs to find a woman's kind of wisdom and courage in her mother. Then she can identify in marvelous ways with her mother, looking ahead with good expectations to years when she will be the mother in a good family.

At the same time, that daughter of yours wants to see in you an intelligent man's viewpoint about life, plus the ability to head up the family in fatherly ways. Then she can really love you as her father as well as a fine man.

Next to the basic physical necessities of life, there is no more fundamental human need than the need for love. There have been too many parents who almost totally lacked genuine love for anyone, even their own children. Such youngsters can become very sick emotionally, unable to cope with life — sometimes even with a great deal of professional help.

Girls, just like boys, need to feel warmly loved and genuinely wanted in the family. How they think their father feels about them is just as important as how they believe their mother feels. Your own daughter needs to know that you are glad she is your youngster. If she knows this, you can be the strictest father in the land and she will not battle you very much. If she doesn't know it — or if you do not love and value her as your child — she probably will interpret your slightest disapproval of anything about her to be as bad as a beating.

You are the most important man in her young life. She ought to be able to build her life according to what she sees in yours:

your kindness toward others who have not been able to get along in life due to no real fault of their own;

your forgiveness that flows freely and does not allow you to hold tight to grudges or revenge;

your wisdom to withhold judgment until all the facts have come into view;

your quiet courage that wells up out of deep faith in God;

your uncommon sense that probably is a mixture of all these traits.

Nobody can show her these facets of a good father nearly as well as you can, if you put your brainpower to it. Her mother can show her the comparable facets of a fine woman, and she can copy them in her own young life. But your example of what a good man is like will be priceless to her . . . even if you sing off tune beside her in the Sunday morning worship.

Most of the important things our children learn come by our examples. Every father is a teacher, whether he knows this or not. If your youngster finds in you a sturdy kind of faith and hope and courage, she will be very apt to develop these same traits by watching you face the difficulties and discouragements with inner strength of spirit.

You must have known fathers who leaned on excuses for not doing a better job with their girls. The real problem in most instances is the gradual shutdown of two-way communication between parent and child. Girls often need to talk things out with fathers who see the universe through a man's eyes and a man's aspirations. This kind of experience provides a good foundation for her own mature perspective of men a few short years ahead. Your youngster ought to learn the most important aspects of the psychology of men from you. One good outcome of such two-way communication about human behavior is warmer mutual respect.

There is a fine art to being available to a youngster who might want to talk to you about what has been troubling her. Of course, she has to know that you love and value her. Otherwise she could not afford to tell you how she really feels about anything important. We rarely confide in anyone we think may not truly care about us. Neither do most of us open up to people who pry. Communication flows most freely when children and parents feel safe and secure with one another.

Teen-agers as well as younger children often need to be able to spill out deeper anxieties and fears. Without safety valves, emotional tensions can rise to such levels that something has to go. Our children are no different from the rest of us in this need. The right words and conversation not only can ventilate the mind and heart and diminish neurotic fear and anguish of spirit, but also can mend and heal.

Pleasant and relaxing excursions with her father can let a girl see what intelligent, mature men really are like. Every girl needs a father she can talk to, argue with, race at a picnic, play ball with in the cool of evening, hug and kiss. These things are worth doing even if you have to make room in your time schedule. She is growing up just as swiftly as you are adding years to yourself. Waiting until next year or the year after that will find her older and that much less inclined to talk or swim or go to the concert with you. Out of these experiences come the kind of deep mutual ties and understanding that have kept thousands of girls right-minded and trustworthy about sex, even in a world where morals and ethics sometimes seem extinct.

Bad behavior in any child often is a symptom of deeper conflicts that are not being met and resolved in intelligent ways. How a child is loved and valued, encouraged and disciplined can greatly affect intelligence and character. Children who are wisely disciplined and encouraged are more likely to learn to think of themselves as capable and resourceful. Their good feelings of self-esteem carry them through such situations with inner poise. Such a girl or boy is not apt to drift toward any kind of delinquency.

Every experienced parent knows that bad behavior in a child rarely happens with no previous signals and no past incidents of disobedience or defiance. There are always signals of trouble ahead. Alert fathers and mothers notice such signals in time to intervene and prevent the youngster from skidding into serious mistakes. I have never known a girl who did not hope her father would keep her from drifting into serious trouble of any kind. Girls just as much as boys want their fathers to help them behave rightly.

Your wisdom in controlling your youngster is one of the best measures of how much you really love and value her. She knows this, whether she has said so in plain words or not. She knows that her mother should have a hand in controlling her too; but you, her father, have an equal share in the job. Your personal examples are very important, too, along with your rules. You won't be able to sell her any double standards on the important issues in life. She will come much closer to following what you do and what you believe than what you say about these issues.

Your daughter does not have to believe that you are the wisest man in all the world to count you as a good father. She does want to be able to come to you with important questions about life. She needs to see that you are learning and growing, too, that you are open to new ideas, new concepts.

Being a real father to your children is one job that no one else can ever do as well as you. Good fathers deserve their full share of top praise, for they are helping to build the loftiest cathedrals in the universe: young hearts and minds that are learning how to make this world a better place in which to live.

TEACH RESPECT AND RESPONSIBILITY

by James Dobson

*Assistant Professor of Pediatrics,
U.S.C. School of Medicine, Los Angeles*

Nature has generously equipped most animals with a fear of things that could be harmful to them, but did not protect the frog quite so well. If a frog is placed in a pan of warm water under which the heat is being increased very gradually, he will typically show no inclination to escape. As the temperature continues to intensify, the frog remains oblivious to his danger; he could easily hop his way to safety, but he is apparently thinking about something else. He will just sit there, contentedly peering over the edge of the pan while the steam curls ominously around his nostrils. Eventually the boiling frog will pass on to his reward, having succumbed to a misfortune he could easily have avoided.

Human beings have some of the same perceptual inadequacies as their little green friends. We quickly become excited about *sudden* dangers that confront us. However, if a threatening problem arises very slowly, perhaps over a decade or two, we often allow ourselves to "boil" in happy ignorance. This blindness to gradual disaster is best illustrated by the way we have ignored the turmoil that is spreading systematically through the younger generation of Americans. We have passively accepted a slowly deteriorating "youth scene" without uttering a croak of protest.

Narcotic and drug usage by America's juveniles is an indescribable shame. A Chicago psychiatrist, Dr. Marvin Schwarz, says: "The kids on heroin all have long histories of drug use." In San Francisco, Dr. Barry Ramer, director of the Study for Special Problems, calls heroin now "the most readily available drug on the streets." He adds: "In my wildest nightmares, I never dreamed of what we are seeing today."

Many young people are now playing another dangerous game, packaged neatly under the title of sexual freedom.

Certainly, illicit sex is not a new phenomenon; this activity has been with us for a few thousand years. However, immorality has not been embraced as right and proper by public figures in America until now. The *"Playboy* philosophy" has been accepted as the banner of the now generation. Whole classes now argue with their teachers about the "rightness" of sexual freedom.

The older generation must assume the blame for allowing the circumstances to deteriorate. There was a time when the trend could easily have been reversed, but like the contented frog, we must have been thinking about something else. The time has come for us to hop, rather than boil.

Many of our difficulties with the present generation of young people began in the tender years of their childhood. There is a critical period during the first four or five years of a child's life when he can be taught proper attitudes. These early concepts become rather permanent. If it is important to produce respectful, responsible young citizens, then we should set out to mold them accordingly. The point is obvious: heredity does not equip a child with proper attitudes; children will learn what they are taught.

Respectful and responsible children result from families where the proper combination of love and discipline is present. An absence of either is often disastrous.

Down through the ages, people have dreamed and longed for a day when their major troubles would be resolved: "If we just didn't have this terrible war to fight; if we could eliminate this famine, or this depression, or this plague . . ." At last in 1950-1970, a generation was born on which all the coveted goodness was heaped. But instead of bringing exuberance and gratitude, there has come antagonism and haughty contempt for the generation that worked to provide it. Why?

The central cause of the turmoil among the young must again be found in the tender years of childhood: we demanded neither respect nor responsible behavior from our children, and it should not be surprising that some of our young citizens are now demonstrating the absence of these virtues.

I am thoroughly convinced that the proper control of children can be found in a reasonable, common sense philosophy, where five key elements are paramount.

1. Developing respect for the parents is the critical factor in child management.

It is most important that a child respect his parents, not for the purpose of satisfying their egos, but because the child's relationship with his parents provides the basis for his attitude toward all other people. His view of parental authority becomes the cornerstone of his later outlook on school authority, police and law, the people with whom he will eventually live and work, and for society in general.

If you want your child to accept your values when he reaches his teen years, then you must be worthy of his respect during his younger days.

This factor is important for Christian parents who wish to "sell" their concept of God to their children. They must first sell themselves. If they are not worthy of respect, then neither is their religion or their morals, or their government, or their country, or any of their values. This becomes the "generation gap" at its most basic level.

The issue of respect can be a useful tool in knowing when to punish and how excited one should get about a given behavior. First, the parent should decide whether an undesirable behavior represents a direct challenge of his authority — to his position as the father or mother. Punishment should depend on that evaluation.

In my opinion, spankings should be reserved for the moment a child (age ten or less) expresses a defiant "I will not!" or "You shut up!" When a youngster tries this kind of stiff-necked rebellion, you had better take it out of him, and pain is a marvelous purifier. It is not the time to have a discussion about the virtues of obedience. It is not the occasion to send him in his room to pout. You have drawn a line in the dirt, and the child has deliberately flopped his big hairy toe across it. Who is going to win? Who has the most courage? Who is in charge here? If you do not answer these questions conclusively for the child, he will precipitate other battles designed to ask them again and again. It is the ultimate paradox of childhood that a youngster wants to be controlled, but he insists that his parents earn the right to control him.

A parent can absolutely destroy a child through the application of harsh, oppressive, whimsical, unloving, or capricious punishment. However, you cannot inflict permanent damage to a child if you follow this technique: identify the rules well in advance; let there be no doubt about what is and is not acceptable behavior; when the child cold-bloodedly chooses to challenge those known boundaries in a haughty manner, give him good reason to regret it; at all times, demonstrate love and affection and kindness and understanding. The parent must convince himself that punishment (as outlined above) is not something he does *to* the child; it is something he does *for* the child. His attitude towards his disobedient youngster is this: "I love you too much to let you behave like that."

Punishment should usually be administered away from the curious eyes of gloating onlookers. The child should not be laughed at unmercifully. His strong feelings and requests, even if foolish, should be given an honest appraisal. A father who is sarcastic and biting in his criticism of children cannot expect to receive genuine respect in return. His offspring might *fear* him enough to conceal their contempt, but revenge will often erupt in late adolescence. Children know the wisdom of the old axiom which recommends: "Don't mock the alligator until you are across the stream." Thus a vicious, toothy father may intimidate his household for a time, but if he does not demonstrate respect for its inhabitants, they may return his hostility when they reach the safety of early adulthood.

Repeating the first point, the most vital objective of disciplining a child is to gain and maintain his respect. If the parents fail in this task, life becomes complicated indeed.

2. The best opportunity to communicate often occurs after punishment.

Nothing brings a parent and child closer together than for the mother or father to win decisively after being defiantly challenged. This is particularly true if the child was "asking for it," knowing full well that he deserved what he got. After the emotional ventilation, the child will often want to crumple to the breast of his parent, and he should be welcomed with open, warm, loving arms. At that moment you can talk heart to heart. You can tell him how much you love him, and how important he is to you. You can explain why he was punished and how he can avoid the difficulty next time. This kind of communication is not made possible by other disciplinary measures, including standing the child in the corner or taking away his fire truck.

3. Control without nagging (it is possible).

Yelling and nagging at children can become a habit, and an ineffectual one at that! Parents often use anger to get action, instead of using action to get action. It doesn't work.

Minor pain can provide excellent motivation for the child. The parent should have some means of making the child want to cooperate, other than simply obeying because he was told to do so.

There will be those among my readers who feel that the deliberate, premeditated application of minor pain to a sweet, little child is a harsh and unloving recommendation. I ask those skeptics to hear me out. Consider the alternatives. On the one hand, there is constant nagging and strife between parent and child. When the youngster discovers there is no threat behind the millions of words he hears, he stops listening to them. The only messages he responds to are those reaching a peak of emotion, which means there is much screaming and yelling going on. But the most important limitation of these verbal reprimands is that their user often has to resort at last to physical punishment, anyway. Thus, instead of the discipline being administered in a calm and judicious manner, the parent has become unnerved and frustrated, swinging wildly at the belligerent child.

One should never underestimate a child's awareness that he is breaking the rules. I think most children are rather analytical about their defiance of adult authority; they consider the deed in advance, weighing its probable consequences. If the odds are too great that justice will triumph, they'll take a safer course.

The parent must recognize that the most successful techniques of control are those which manipulate something important to the child. Minor pain is one of those important variables. Words following words carry little or no motivational power for the child.

4. Don't saturate the child with excessive materialism.

Many American children are inundated with excesses that work toward their detriment. It has been said that prosperity offers a greater test of character than does adversity, and I'm inclined to agree. There are few conditions that inhibit a sense of appreciation more than for a child to feel he is entitled to whatever he wants, whenever he wants it. Although it sounds paradoxical, you actually cheat him of pleasure when you give him too much.

Pleasure occurs when an intense need is satisfied. If there is no need, there is no pleasure. A glass of water is worth more than gold to a man dying of thirst. The analogy to children should be obvious. If you never allow a child to want something, he never enjoys the pleasure of receiving it. If you buy him a tricycle before he can walk, and a bicycle before he can ride, and a car before he can drive, and a diamond ring before he knows the value of money, he accepts these gifts with little pleasure and less appreciation. How unfortunate that such a child never had the chance to long for something, dreaming about it at night and plotting for it by day. I suggest that you allow your child the thrill of temporary deprivation; it's more fun and much less expensive.

5. Avoid extremes in control and love.

There is little question about the consequences of disciplinary extremes. On the side of harshness, a child suffers the humiliation of total domination. The atmosphere is icy and rigid, and he lives in constant fear. He is unable to make his own decisions and his personality is squelched beneath the hobnailed boot of parental authority. The opposite position, ultimate permissiveness, is equally tragic. Under this setting, the child is his own master from his earliest babyhood. He thinks the world revolves around his heady empire, and he often has utter contempt and disrespect for those closest to him. Anarchy and chaos reign in his home. Both extremes are disastrous. There is safety only in the middle ground, which is sometimes difficult to locate.

The overprotective parent finds it difficult to allow a child to take reasonable risks; those risks are a necessary prelude to maturity. Likewise, the materialistic problems are often maximized in a family where the children are so badly needed by one or both parents. Prolonged emotional immaturity is another frequent consequence of overprotection.

The "middle ground" of love and control must be sought if we are to produce healthy, responsible children.

I am recommending a simple principle: when you are defiantly challenged, win decisively. When the child's actions ask, "Who's in charge?" show him. When he mutters, "Who loves me?" take him in your arms and surround him with affection. Treat him with respect and dignity, and expect the same from him. Then begin to enjoy the sweet benefits of competent parenthood.

The most effective guard against delinquency is a father who is at the same time both strict and loving.

—SHELDON GLUECK

A FATHER'S RIGHTS AND OBLIGATIONS

by J. H. Waterink

Psychologist and Retired Professor,
Free University of Amsterdam

In a family consisting of a father, mother, and four children, a vinegar bottle was broken to smithereens. When the father came into the kitchen and saw the broken bottle, he raised his voice of authority and said to his eleven-year-old son, "Don't deny that you broke that bottle, Bob. Get out of my sight and go to bed. This will cost you your afternoon's outing."

The boy tensed his muscles, looked his father in the eye and said, "You are wrong, Father. I did not break that bottle."

Upon this the father replied, "Keep still! If I say you are to go to bed, you are to go to bed. Now don't argue."

The boy responded with dignified calmness, "If you send me to bed, you are being unjust, and injustice is sinful."

"If you didn't break the bottle, then go to bed because of your impudence!"

The boy tried to reason with his father, "Look, Father, you could have been mistaken about the bottle; but you can never say that I am being impudent. You are angry at me without a cause, therefore I am not going to bed."

This sent his father into a rage, and then Mother appeared on the scene. In the resultant conflict between Father and Mother, the minister was called into consultation. He tried to justify both the father and mother, and finally they came to me for counseling.

The father stated his case in this manner: "Apart from the question of whether I was right or wrong about the vinegar bottle, Bob must respect my authority. That is his duty and I have a right to demand that respect from him. My wife has no right to interfere, even if she feels that Bob is somewhat justified."

In answer to the question of whether or not a child must

recognize his father's authority, I answered unhesitatingly, "Yes, he must do so."

The father turned to his wife and said, "See, I'm right."

I then said to the father, "Look here. The whole question of respect for authority has nothing to do with the uproar you occasioned at your home. You are completely mistaken about the issue you raised. You should ask yourself to what extent a child is duty bound to obey his parents when they misuse their power." The father looked at me questioningly, whereupon I proceeded, "You accused Bob of breaking the bottle. Were you sure that he had done so?"

"No," said the father, "but I could surmise that."

I asked, "How?"

"I saw him hurrying from the kitchen just as I came along," replied the man.

I shall not repeat the remainder of the conversation, but I tried to make clear to the father that he had grossly misused his authority. Certainly, a father has authority over his child; but that authority does not give him the right to send his child to bed and deprive him of an afternoon's outing on the strength of a mistaken assumption that he had done wrong. Further, he does not have the slightest right to call "impudence" his son's honest statement of his father's mistake. Through the whole affair Bob maintained an entirely proper demeanor, as the father himself later admitted. The father's insistence that the child was duty bound to recognize his authority was little more than an effort to vindicate his own behavior and to cover his own rash demeanor with a cloak of dogma.

I relate this incident because it illustrates a universal question — to what limits may parents go in demanding absolute obedience from their children? It is an extremely important question.

Let me begin by saying that when this question is so clearly and consciously asked, usually something has already gone wrong. Where the situation is good and relationships are as they ought to be, such a question seldom needs to be raised.

That is true in other areas of life as well. When differences rise concerning the exact duties of a husband versus those of his wife, when they are concerned about the limits of his authority over her, when a wife wants to know what she may do without consulting her husband — usually something is not quite right between them.

Bob, the boy in the above case, had long sensed the strain though he was only eleven years old, and had discussed it with his oldest sister's fiancé. Later Bob said to me, "I do not want to become like my father, and I feel that if I always bow beneath his whip I shall become just like him. I don't want to do that in any event." Bob remained so calm because he had prepared himself for just such an event. Besides, Bob was an extremely bright and likeable boy.

But if we recognize that matters have already gone amiss when one raises the question, a clarification of the limits of parental authority may have its value.

Permit me to make just this observation: we must be very careful in speaking of our rights. People who constantly refer to their rights tread on dangerous ground. Is it true that you have the unqualified right to the respect of your children, and that you have every right to exercise authority over your children? No, you certainly do not have an "unqualified right." You can never sever that right from your parental duty before God. Calvin states it beautifully: "Does a person demand his rights? Certainly, I am prepared to grant him his rights, but in so doing I shall say that he has no other rights than the rights to fulfill his duties."

From this it follows that, as soon as you do not perform your duty, your right immediately vanishes. Bob's father disregarded his duty when he unjustly accused his son of something which he had not done; and at that moment he forfeited his right to respect for his parental authority.

Parents, perform your parental duty toward God and toward your children. Then, and then only, can you speak of your parental rights.

There are cases in which parents endanger their own authority by carrying it out beyond reasonable limits.

Keith, a fourteen-year-old boy, was expected to go to bed at nine-thirty. Well and good; if this is the rule in that family, he must go to bed at nine-thirty. But on a certain evening Keith, who was in his second year of high school, was studying for an examination to be given the next day. He was still working at nine-thirty when his father interrupted him. "Keith, it's nine-thirty. Go to bed."

"Oh, Father," said Keith, "I didn't realize it was so late. I'm not quite finished reviewing. Give me just another fifteen minutes and I'll be finished."

"No!" said his father. "A rule is a rule, and nine-thirty is your bedtime."

"Yes," replied Keith, "but, really, I need just fifteen minutes. I have only three more pages to review."

"Give me that book," shouted his father, "and go to bed."

This father exceeded the limits of his authority. The rule "nine-thirty is bedtime" is no God-given command. It is a father's duty to teach his son a sense of responsibility and self-discipline. That is much more important than going to bed fifteen minutes earlier or later.

Much is being said about the rebellious spirit of children and young people. On the one hand, this spirit of rebellion has come about because children have never learned respect for authority as their parents did not exercise authority; on the other hand, it is also possible that they did not learn respect for authority because the parents misused it. Both are equally dangerous. It is no wonder that there are so many pitfalls in the exercising of authority: he who wields authority wields a God-given weapon, and he must constantly be on guard lest he misuse it for selfish ends. Authority must never be exercised in an arbitrary, unreasonable manner.

Father or mother must never take a "high-and-mighty" attitude. Authority can be properly and profitably exercised only when the authority figure knows himself to be dependent upon the authority of God and his Word. This is true of the exercise of all authority, but especially of parental authority.

There is one more point, and it is the heart of the questions we are treating.

Authority over children, especially by parents, is true authority only when it is inseparable from the exercise of love. And love is longsuffering; love does not think evil; and love vaunteth not itself. He who prayerfully practices loving authority in bringing up his children is not likely to have too much of a problem in knowing the bounds of authority.

So don't let these problems bother you unduly. But devote yourself prayerfully, with all your heart, to being a good parent to your children. They in turn will devote themselves in love to you and will feel safeguarded under your authority.

4

The Man and His Business

YOU AND YOUR JOB

by Bruce Larson

President, Faith At Work

How do you see your job? The attitude you have about your work reveals a great deal about faith. The Bible indicates that every Christian ought to feel a sense of vocation in his work. If you are miserable or bored in your work, or dread going to it, then God is speaking to you. He either wants to change the job you are in or — more likely — he wants to change *you*.

Remember the story about the blind man whom Jesus healed? After our Lord touched his eyes, Jesus asked the man what he saw. He reported that he saw "men as trees walking." When he had received a second touch from the Master, he saw men clearly. I suspect that many of us need a "second touch" by Christ to see our jobs in their right perspective.

A friend in Illinois had joined a small group of seekers meeting for prayer and Bible study and the sharing of their faith each week. Although he had come a long way in his Christian commitment, each week he complained about the customers in his store — how unfair they were, how demanding, and how they took advantage of him.

But one day this man received a "second touch" by God and began to see the people who came into his store —

whether to buy a package of nails or a washing machine — as people sent by God. He anticipated each sale as an adventure in personal relationships.

At Christmas time, with all the rush of increased sales, this man said to the group one night in amazement, "You know, what surprises me is how the people in this town have changed. Last Christmas they were rude, pushy, and demanding, but this year I haven't had a difficult customer in my store! Everyone is understanding and trying his best to cooperate." They all laughed. They knew the change had not been in the town but in the storekeeper.

But in a more profound way, perhaps the change was also in the town. As we see people through the eyes of faith, they actually do change. They respond to us almost directly in proportion to the amount of love we have for them as people.

Let me suggest five questions each of us should periodically ask ourselves about our job.

1. Why am I here in this job? Do you feel you are in your present job because of an accident? Because you happened to answer an ad, or your brother-in-law got tired of having you sit around and found you a job? Because of ambition? These attitudes certainly undercut any sense of Christian vocation. We should feel we are in our work because God has called us to it, in just as real a way as he has called any bishop, clergyman, or priest.

Several months ago a man asked me to call on him in his large office in New York City. He said, "A year ago I turned my life over to Jesus Christ. It happened in my church." He then described the change that had begun to happen in his home — new communication between him and his wife, deeper understanding of his teen-age daughter. There were many other evidences of his new commitment.

Then he said, "I find now, a year later, that I am still behind the same desk doing the same job in the same way, and I suspect something is wrong. If Christ has come in as Lord of my life, things ought to be very different in what I do eight or ten hours a day." He was right, of course.

Now he is exploring, along with some other men, the opportunities and strategy for Christian ministry in daily work.

We must dispense with the myth that commitment to Christ means becoming a clergyman, or that work done inside a church building or in a church organization is more holy, somehow, than work done in the marketplace. Christ came to give us a sense of calling in everyday work. This is where the world is changed, and where the kingdom is built.

Jesus himself was a working man and he called twelve working men to be his initial disciples. He could have been born into a priestly family, but he was not. We must understand the really radical thing God has done in Jesus Christ, in wanting to build a new world and a new kingdom primarily through committed working men.

2. *For whom am I working?* Are you working for God, or for men? You cannot really serve both. When we are addicted to people's praise and thanks and rewards, we are in a real way under the tyranny of men and are working for them.

When we work for God, we are free to serve others no matter how unreasonable or thankless they may be. Our reward is God himself saying to us, "Well done, good and faithful servant."

We need continually to ask ourselves whether we are willing to risk our jobs and our financial security in obedience to Jesus Christ. When we really work for God and know that it is he to whom we are responsible and from whom we get our reward, we are then free to be his people in any given situation.

3. *What am I working for?* Wages? Prestige? Or am I working to do the will of God? This has much to say about our motives.

Christ's own life gives us a key. When he found people abusing others in the temple, he came in and violently upset the status quo. But when people wished to destroy *him,* he let them drive nails into his hands. Perhaps this is the kind of freedom Christian men need in their jobs; not to protect their own interests but to look to the interests of others; to protest when innocent people are being hurt but not to protest for self-preservation. This freedom comes only when we can answer the question, "What am I working for?" with: "To do the will of God."

Where is your security? Is it in the person who pays your salary, or do you see him only as an agent whom God at this time has chosen to supply your needs? You cannot really love your boss or paymaster until you see him as God's agent. If you see *him* as your provider, then you cannot be honest with him, and fear and resentment are bound to color your relationship.

I have a wonderful Chinese friend, Moses Chow. His father was one of two sons in a family in pre-Communist China. He had become a Christian and was told by his father that if he persisted in following this "new god" he would be disinherited.

There was wealth in the family, but Mr. Chow could choose only the way of life and life abundant. In his determination to follow Jesus Christ, he was disinherited and he left China.

Moses Chow said his father made a new home in a new country in the Far East and has been quite successful as a Christian businessman. He left the security of the world and trusted God, who was able to provide. Meanwhile, Moses' grandfather and others fell victim to Communism and lost everything. We don't follow God because he makes us secure, but our security is in God — even in economic matters.

4. With whom am I working? God wants us to be aware always of the people next to us. It's not enough to work honestly and industriously, for Christ calls us to be a priesthood of believers who willingly take responsibility for those who are our neighbors.

God calls the laity to do a job the clergy cannot do in many instances. In a parish I once served, a close friend who was a doctor became quite ill. Though I visited him almost daily, I saw no improvement and no benefit from my visits. One day I went to see this Christian doctor and found him greatly improved and free from fear.

I asked him what had happened, and he told me of a visit a few hours before with a senior surgeon in the area who had prayed with him and given him a prescription. The prescription was to read Joshua 1:9. My friend had been touched by God, and not through a clergyman but through a brother physician.

5. *What kind of place am I in?* Jesus Christ, by his very call to accept him as Lord and Savior, has brought us inside a revolutionary movement so that the place we are in assumes tremendous importance.

No job is so menial that it is unimportant to a Communist! Shouldn't this be true for any Christian trying to build a worldwide kingdom? Christians should ask God to show them the nature of the place they are in. How important is the particular store, shop, industry, or service which is theirs? What could God do through that particular organization to change his world?

There is a revolution going on in the world. Jesus Christ himself is the leader, and when we accept him as our Lord, he calls us into it with him. He needs us. He wants us to see our jobs with the eyes of faith and understanding as something far more than a means of earning a livelihood. Our jobs are places where, as revolutionaries, we help to accomplish his revolution in the hearts and lives of men everywhere.

Unless the job means more than the pay it will never pay more.

—H. BERTRAM LEWIS

SPELL IT W-O-R-K

by D. P. Luben

Author and Lecturer

The first man was sent forth out of a "workless garden" and admonished, "In the sweat of thy face shalt thou eat bread."

Work! The all-time best seller mentions it over three hundred fifty times.

Work — the first commandment of success.

When the eminently qualified Charles M. Schwab, great American steel magnate, wrote his "Ten Commandments of Success," he put hard work at the very top of the list. "Work hard. Hard work is the best investment a man can make."

Thomas A. Edison, labeled "The Wizard of Menlo Park" because of the seemingly magical succession of his inventions, denied that he was a genius in any sense of the word; and attributed his success to dedicated work.

George Bernard Shaw said, "When I was a young man, I observed that nine out of ten things I did were failures. I didn't want to be a failure, so I did ten times more work!"

And current successes sing the same song.

"What counts most is how hard you work."

"Luck is what you make it. You have to work."

Although "getting along with people" is known to be a most important requisite, there are people on top who don't know how. Though a good education is invaluable, there are uneducated millionaires. In every calling we can see leaders and winners who possess no special talent or ability. The name of the game these people play? Work. It's the one common denominator of success.

Hard work has no stand-in and no successor. Cultivate good relations with others, but work. Study as much as you can, but work. And if your talents and natural abilities are sparse, work harder. Fortunes are found in everyday pains. Give, if you want the generous gains.

Booker T. Washington, the educator, knew how to give. At sixteen he traveled five hundred miles to attend college. When he arrived, a teacher at the institute ordered him to sweep the room. He swept it "characteristically" — as one biographer says — three times! And dusted four!

Not guilty of the great misconception, Booker Washington realized he wasn't sweeping that room for the teacher but for himself. He assured his acceptance.

Years later Professor Washington, founder of the Tuskegee Norman and Industrial Institute of Alabama, proved again that we work for ourselves. As he was walking past a southern mansion, the lady of the house called out for him to chop some wood. Without hesitation he pulled off his coat, chopped the wood, and carried it into the house. One of the servant girls recognized him and enlightened her mistress. Next morning the rich Mrs. Varner ordered her carriage, drove to the educator's office, and apologized. Furthermore, she thereafter gave money to support his institution and influenced many of her wealthy friends to do the same.

In the amazing life of Helen Keller, the worth of the work of the "miracle worker," Anne Sullivan, is undeniable. Constant and extensive exertion by this dedicated teacher truly transformed a desperate, despondent child into a valuable human being. Only time can share the credit.

As the winning worker soon learns, time is his best ally. He will not misuse it; nor will he kill his chances by killing it. He makes every minute of every working hour productive. And he sometimes steals from his allotment for sleep and play.

Edison stole steadily from his sleep allotment. According to his son, Charles, he rarely slept more than four hours a night. Too much sleep at a time, he claimed, "makes you dopey. You lose time, vitality, and opportunities."

Plato said, "Nothing is more unworthy of a wise man or ought to trouble him more than to have allowed more time for trifling and useless things than they deserved."

The people of Plato's *Republic* had twenty-four hours a

day to manage toward their goals. And so do we. But we possess heretofore inconceivable advantages: we command a whole crew of time-saving devices.

The automobile whisks us to our place of business (barring traffic jams) ten times faster. But how do we utilize the saved time? Work longer and get more done? Or sleep longer? Tarry over two or three cups of coffee instead of one? Read the entire morning paper in lieu of the headlines?

The company computer shrinks to a fraction the time formerly required for its many functions. And it bequeaths the rest to increase production, branch out, or conquer new horizons. But how do we capitalize on it? Close earlier? Take Friday afternoons off? Don't bother to come in at all on Saturdays? Declare more holidays?

For centuries civilized men have gradually been working fewer and fewer of their twenty-four hours. Even Benjamin Franklin's ingenious idea of daylight saving time, finally put into effect during World War I, failed to turn the trend. We gained one more hour of daylight, but we didn't *use* one more hour.

Today "Six days thou shalt labor" is interpreted to mean only, "Don't work on the seventh" — while millions find it a struggle to render even the required five work days each week. And we call it progress!

You bet! The languid have it made; the zealous have it easy; and the cost of "success" goes down, down, down. That which cost eighteen to twenty hours of hard work in "the good old days" now may be had for approximately ten. But still, at any ratio, work remains the power for progress.

Accordingly, it pays to protect your source of power. No matter how great your expectations or inspirations, if your physical partner lets you down, if your body fails to cooperate or quits, you're liable to lose the race.

Those who win in spite of ill health are rare. Those who lose because of it are countless. Why not insure triumph? Safeguard that most important machine in your operation. Immunize yourself against those ready rebels of worry and tension with a well-managed life; and prevent lost time and costly repair bills with good food, good care, and good habits. Keep your working machine in tip-top condition; then you can work it hard.

From Hippocrates to the Mayo brothers, medical authorities have asserted that hard work won't hurt us. Back in about 400 B.C. the father of medicine averred, "All parts of the body which are designed for a definite use are kept in health and in enjoyment of fair growth and of long youth by the fulfillment of that use, by their suitable exercise in the duty for which they were made."

And Dr. Charles Mayo said, "Worry . . . profoundly affects the health," but, "I have never known a man who died from overwork."

So put forth!

Effort is the great effecter; many a mediocre man by worldly standards attained great heights with little else.

Once a handy man whose job included locking the plant doors after working hours found one of the locks broken. How could he secure the building? He sat by that door all night. He worked all night. Extra effort became a habit; the handy man became a wealthy industrialist.

In Missouri a beautiful $20,000 house was built in its entirety, design, masonry, carpentry, plumbing, and finishing, by a gang of hard-working high school boys! They had little learning and less experience. They used effort.

In 1949 an unknown virologist started research on poliomyelitis, just another job in his field. But he worked on it sixteen to eighteen hours a day, six days a week, for five years. The ultimate discovery of a polio preventive made history and placed the name of Dr. Jonas Salk with the world's great men of medicine.

The wonders of work make history. Enough work effects "miracles." The decree for planet Earth is: "In the sweat of thy face shalt thou eat bread."

How much bread do *you* want?

LAWS OF BUSINESS SUCCESS

by Louis M. Grafe

*Late Advertising Manager of the
Institute of Mentalphysics, Inc.*

Is there a Law of Success? There is. Can we learn what it is? We can. Why do not successful men let us know what the law is? Because such men themselves do not know what it is; for a time, they simply live by it unconsciously. I found the law in the Bible, the greatest of all books. I saw it repeatedly in the Bible for many years before I realized its true meaning. As given there, the first rule is: "Whosoever will be great among you, let him be your minister; and whosoever will be chief among you, let him be your servant" (Matthew 20:26, 27). Finally it dawned upon me that this did not mean that I should drop the kind of work at which I was skilled and become a domestic servant or a preacher. What it did mean was this:

Success Rule 1: Whosoever will be great among you, let him minister unto the people's needs; and whosoever will be chief among you, let him give service in that field in which he is most skilled.

Do the great become so really by ministering to the people's needs? Washington, Lincoln, and many others became great that way. Henry Ford, in developing an automobile and a mass production system by which it could be offered people at a low price, became great by "ministering unto the people's needs." The same is true of other great industrialists, as well as of your locally successful merchants and manufacturers. The more people they minister to, the greater they are. Washington and Lincoln ministered, not only to their contemporaries, but to many generations since.

But how about the "chiefs" among us, those who are not great, but still fairly successful? Do they become so by "giving service in that field in which they are most skilled"? Their service is often not to the masses of the people, I admit, but they do give service to a limited group or class. This is true of the successful businessmen, physicians, lawyers, superintendents, managers, artists, writers, and educators. If they attain any degree of success, they do so by giving service in the field in which they are most skilled. They may not become great, but they do rise above the common level and become "chiefs" among us.

We can now proceed to the next rule in the Law of Success. In the Bible I found two commandments which were said to contain all the law and the prophets. The first is outside our province here, but the second is, "Love thy neighbor as thyself." Most people understand this as meaning that we should have a good feeling toward our neighbor, a kind of inward glow. But that pleasant feeling is mere delusion, make-believe, unless it is expressed through service — only then is it love. Did the good Samaritan simply smile kindly at the stranger in distress, sympathize with him, and pass on? No, he stopped to serve him. Love without service is no love at all; service is its only measure. Thoughts such as these led me to what I believe is the true meaning of the second commandment:

Success Rule 2: Serve thy neighbor as thyself.

Did Henry Ford serve his neighbor as he would himself? I can imagine him saying to himself as he started out, "If I were a man of modest means, what kind of car would I like to have . . . what price would I be able to pay . . . how long would I have to use the car . . . how much upkeep expense could I afford?" Then he proceeded to serve his neighbor just as he would serve himself if he were in the same position. Only a man with whom service is a passion would supply parts for cars twelve and fourteen years old, as the Ford Company does. I can hear Ford saying to himself, "If I were a poor man, forced to buy an eight-year-old car at second- or third-hand, in what condition would I want it to be . . . how long would I continue to need parts for it . . .

how much gasoline could I afford to buy?" Unexpected rewards for service freely and eagerly given are what make men deservedly rich.

You do not have to be a merchant or manufacturer to follow the two rules already given. You can follow them in whatever job you hold. The employee of the merchant serves the customers just as the merchant himself does. The employee serves also his employer. He serves his wife and children by providing for them. Much of this kind of service cannot bring complete success, though it may enable one to keep the wolf from the door. But if service alone will not bring success, what more is required?

For one thing, efficiency is required — efficiency in service. The parable of the ten talents ends with this quotation: "For unto every one that hath shall be given, and he shall have abundance; but from him that hath not shall be taken even that which he hath." Let me make it clearer by paraphrasing:

Success Rule 3: "For unto every efficient one shall be given, and he shall have abundance; but from him that is not efficient shall be taken away all the talents and all the money which he hath."

Efficiency is not a matter of knowledge only, but a matter of feeling and spirit. "And whatsoever ye do, do it heartily, as to the Lord, and not unto men" (Colossians 3:23). We must be passionately devoted to giving better service. Whatever we do must be done heartily, as if we are serving God instead of men. We must be fervent and enthusiastic; we must be watchful and alert to improve ourselves and our service. And all this must be done, not for an hour or a day, a week or a month, but for year upon year. I can see my readers, right now, throwing up their hands and exclaiming, "But I am not built that way. I cannot maintain fervency or enthusiasm all day long for year upon year." To tell the truth, no one can unless there is an intense and sustained feeling that drives him on, a feeling that never lets him rest unless he is up and doing. He is driven — often in spite of the will — by emotions that force him into constant effort. This leads to:

Success Rule 4: One cannot drive himself to success; one must *be driven* by a dominant, constant, and enduring emotion or mood.

Without this dominant emotion, the best of resolutions, the most intelligent of plans, the keenest of inspirations will never be carried out. The mere knowledge that a dominant emotion may drive you to success does not automatically give you such a dynamo of power.

Where and how can you attain it? Briefly, the answer is: choose the dominant emotion most likely to drive you to success; and cultivate that emotion constantly.

We shall begin with the emotions which sometimes lead to success but which I do not recommend. The first is greed or lust for power. Unquestionably, this is the driving force behind many apparently successful men. Usually, as in the case of a Napoleon, Hitler, or Mussolini, they overreach themselves and end in failure.

The second is fear of poverty. This is the driving force behind many moderately successful men. It leads many a man to learn a trade or profession and work reasonably hard at his job, but no man ever achieved substantial success through fear of poverty.

The third is pride. Envy, the spirit of rivalry, the desire to "keep up with the Joneses" undoubtedly inspires prodigious effort in some people and leads them to a success they might not achieve otherwise. But the use of pride as a chief motive is dangerous. For short bursts of effort, as in an athletic contest, a lawsuit, a "drive" of any kind, it is stimulating. But for the long pull, pride, like the desire for security, is a coin with a counterfeit side — fear of shame or humiliation. Cultivated continuously, pride would degenerate into this fear and lead to changeableness and inefficiency.

Now consider a motive which I do recommend. I doubt, however, that many can energize themselves with it continuously without special gifts or talents. The name I give this motive is: love of work.

This is the motive that goads the great artist, the great scientist, the genius in all fields, to untiring and incessant effort. He is so inflamed with zeal that his work becomes a joy, an ecstasy. No sacrifice of toil or study or time, no sacrifice of self or others, is of moment if only the great work be forwarded. The same near-mania for his work, his business, his factory, often energizes the successful businessman. He is driven to success by the joy of creation.

There is danger in such an impelling force. The man activated by it to a high degree is inclined to be unbalanced. He will brook no opposition and will therefore take great hazards, both with the law and his fortune. As a result he sometimes ends in bankruptcy, sometimes in the toils of the law, sometimes in domestic tragedy caused by neglect of his family. Most of us, however, are not inclined to have such an overwhelming love for our work; consequently, we can cultivate that valuable source of energy without fear.

But it is against ordinary human nature to love work for work's sake. The chances are you will have to love work for the sake of something else. The something else will then be your dominant emotion. What can it be? Though there are many other emotions which occasionally drive men to success, only two are so frequently effective as to deserve mention here. These are: love of people; and love of God.

Success Rule 5: Cultivate a love of people until your greatest desire is to make them happy. When this desire becomes an enduring passion for serving them, you will be *driven* to do everything necessary to success.

In short, only those passionately devoted to giving more or better service, always to more people, can ordinarily expect success; and such devotion can best be inspired by love for the people to whom the service is rendered.

Here is the dominant emotion we have been looking for, the one that is without danger to your mental well-being, the one that is in harmony with every law of God and man, the one that can subordinate conflicting emotions which otherwise lead to inefficiency, and the one which will supply the driving force necessary to long-continued application and inspired effort.

It must not be thought that love for people can be cultivated only through social activities; it can be strengthened in the ordinary contacts of your business or employment. The merchant mingles with the customers in his store, the executive with his employees, the salesman with prospects and customers. Each through constant association learns to love his clientele, to enjoy making people happy through his service, and, if he is to be a success, to devote himself passionately to the finding of ways and means by which ever-increasing numbers may likewise be made happy.

Nearly every great success involves sacrifice and prodigious effort possible only to a man dominated by a strong and lasting emotion — usually a love of people that attracts them to him and a strong devotion to serving them that never lets the man rest. They are the greatest artists of all — the artists of service.

But there is one more dominant emotion: it is religious zeal, or love of God. Divided loyalties can tear a man to pieces, can arouse an emotional conflict which makes efficiency impossible. But undivided loyalty can give him godlike strength and power — then we have a Joan of Arc, a Lincoln, a Garibaldi, a Florence Nightingale, a Moses, a Paul. The way to a completely inspired, completely successful life is to lose all sense of self and surrender completely to a Great Loyalty.

Such surrender puts the greatest force in the universe behind your efforts. Laziness becomes impossible. Emotional conflicts that interfere with your efficiency dissolve. Indecision, vacillation are swept aside. You become a *man with a mission*. All emotions fall into line to support the great emotion. Complete harmony, the strength of an integrated personality, follows.

We are driven irresistibly forward in the mainstream of life itself, achieving distinction and success because they are necessary to the great plan of our Creator, when we become important factors in God's plan, an essential part of the Driving Force. Your daily work, your job through which you serve your fellowmen directly or indirectly, should be a part of your faith, should have religious fervor put into it, should become the supreme mission of your life. If your work is a service, that is easy. If it is a *dis*service, find another job or another business that uses service as a vehicle.

You need not worry about money; that will be a natural result. And you will accept that money not because you are greedy, but because it enables you to continue your service, because its accumulation enables you to *give more service* to *more and more people* as the years go by.

A WINNER

A Winner respects those who are superior to him and tries to learn something from them; a Loser resents those who are superior and rationalizes their achievements.

A Winner explains; a Loser explains away.

A Winner says, "Let's find a way"; a Loser says, "There is no way."

A Winner goes through a problem; a Loser tries to go around it.

A Winner says, "There should be a better way to do it"; a Loser says, "That's the way it's always been done here."

A Winner shows he's sorry by making up for it; a Loser says, "I'm sorry," but does the same thing next time.

A Winner knows what to fight for and what to compromise on; a Loser compromises on what he shouldn't, and fights for what isn't worth fighting about.

A Winner works harder than a loser, and has more time; a Loser is always "too busy" to do what is necessary.

A Winner is not afraid of losing; a Loser is secretly afraid of winning.

A Winner makes commitments; a Loser makes promises.
　　　　　　　　　　　　　—AN UNKNOWN WINNER

BECOMING A MANAGER

from Royal Bank of Canada Monthly Letter

In Sir Walter Scott's *Kenilworth,* Queen Elizabeth gave Walter Raleigh a diamond ring, with which he wrote on a window pane: "Fain would I climb, but that I fear to fall." The Queen completed the couplet: "If thy mind fail thee, do not climb at all."

To be an efficient manager does not demand high education, but it does require common sense, keen intelligence, and qualities of judgment, temperament, and drive. In whatever post you reach you must welcome the call to combat the difficulties imposed by problems. You hold your post only as a sportsman holds a challenge cup.

If you are not a natural leader whom others instinctively trust, now is the time to start cultivating the qualities that will raise you into that class.

The pathway to management is much like the hard road followed by a recruit in the armed services pursuing a sergeant's stripes. He has to work at menial tasks; differentiate his left foot from his right; be at the proper place at the assigned time; separate a gun into its component parts, shake them up in a blanket, and put them together again; get along with a mixed bag of other servicemen, including sergeants; learn to help and to accept help; keep healthy; grouch with discretion; develop aptitudes; scorn weakness; grow accustomed to command by obeying and learn how to lead by following others.

Interest in succeeding is the motive power that will see you through the drudgery and tribulations. You have an end in view, and you accept the means to that end.

AMBITION

If you have ambition, difficulty is not an obstacle to progress, but a sure doorway to opportunity. It screens out the amateur, the playboy, and the less able.

Not all the stopwatch systematization in the world will

be worthwhile unless a man's spirit is blazing with aspiration. This is not made up of a desire to hold power, but to develop the department into something better, to see good plans germinate and grow.

Pride of achievement in your present job is a powerful incentive. Here is something you can tie yourself to when other motivations have failed or have lost their strength.

Any person who wishes to become a manager will find starting opportunities right at his elbow. He is a participating member in the success of the firm for which he works. His start toward management occurs when he soaks himself in the facts relating to his job and the managerial job he seeks.

Learn to shift your viewpoint year by year, keeping up with new knowledge and new thoughts.

PROFESSIONAL OUTLOOK

Once a man embarks upon management he must cultivate the attributes of a professional. Some of the marks of a "pro" are: he does not accept mediocrity; he continues his education so as to keep his performance up to date; he accepts the ethical rules of the game; he keeps looking for better ways to do things; he seeks opportunities to expand and display his skill; he is open-minded; and he is fair in his dealings with people.

There is a self-disciplinary cost involved. Refusal to make personal sacrifices for his job holds back many a man. As Cassius said to Brutus in *Julius Caesar:* "Men at some time are masters of their fates; the fault, dear Brutus, is not in our stars, but in ourselves, that we are underlings."

The manager must trust his own judgment. A man's self-confidence measures the height of his possibilities, and no man ever passes his own self-imposed limitation.

ANALYZE, ANALYZE

One infallible rule for clear thinking in any job will carry over into wise management: analyze the situation. Unless you put a problem into words, you do not give it form, and if it is formless it does not exist in a shape that permits solution.

Ideas and conceptions which seem utterly chaotic when circling and colliding in our minds become clear and separated into orbits and systems when we write them or sketch them on paper. There is in the very act of taking a pen in hand something imperative which the most wandering mind seldom resists.

Keeping records of progress may be a nuisance, but so are many of the other things you have to do in preparing for a management position. No aspiring young man should be content unless his personal bookkeeping informs him of his gains and losses. The path of business is littered with the wreckage of men who might have been great if they had done a competent job of cost-accounting.

ADD EXPERIENCE

Get experience where you are, and reach out for more experience on the periphery of your job. Experience helps you to do things. When you get to be a manager you will have this point by which to judge subordinates; do they come to you with decisions or do they expect you to make decisions for them? On the way up you will be judged by the same criterion. Now is the time to practice what you will expect of others.

Fortunately for us, we do not need to confine ourselves to our own experiences. It would be a dreadful prospect if every child entering the world had to wait and learn by experience the burning quality of fire, how to catch and cook his own dinner, and that he cannot tackle a lion barehanded.

The man who depends upon his own experiences has relatively few materials to work with. That is why trade papers, textbooks, and biographies are useful — to make available to us knowledge of the techniques and practices used effectively by others.

This is something that can be learned on the most humble job. If you are a creative pace-setter in your present work, you have the makings of a creative-coach in a managerial job.

To be creative means finding means to improve the job and your part in it. From there you will go on to make trial runs beyond your daily job. You will imagine a problem that might arise in your work — or in your boss's work — and solve it. This is far and away better than finding faults and pointing out difficulties.

The most degrading poverty in a human being — and the greatest obstacle in the way of the person who seeks promotion — is poverty of the imagination. To raise new questions and new possibilities requires creative imagination and marks real advancement. Do not be afraid of allowing your mind to take flights of fancy.

COMMUNICATE CLEARLY

The person aspiring to management level must — and it is an imperative — develop his effectiveness in communication. This includes ease, clarity, and appropriateness of what he says and writes and the thoroughness with which he listens.

Faulty communication has much to do with the disorder in offices and factories. It is not communicating if you merely tell something so that it can be heard. The language and depth of thought must be adapted to the receptive system of the hearers.

You have the obligation to be intelligible. Make no mistake about this: every communication a manager makes does two things; it conveys ideas, and it generates feelings. The receiver's feelings, needs, and motives must be considered as well as his intelligence.

Listening is important. By listening, we reduce misunderstanding, argument, and conflict. We also draw to our advantage on the experiences and opinions of others.

Proper communication is part of cooperation. Every person should develop his capability to walk alone if need be, but he should guard against making self-dependency an obsession. Cooperation within your group, your office, or your workshop is vital to your survival as a manager and to the success of your enterprise.

THREE BUILDING BLOCKS

The aspiring manager will profit by cultivating patience, modesty, and enjoyment of work.

Patience in business includes being big enough to see your suggestions pulled apart by a committee without becoming upset; waiting for an idea that is clear to you to take hold in a superior's mind; going back to a discarded plan to see what can be salvaged, revised, or revitalized; and listening without petulance to a colleague whose contribution to a discussion is incoherent and confused.

As to modesty, wear every promotion lightly. A man may ruin his prospects by throwing his weight around when he is given a little authority. Take delight in effective action rather than domination, and do not try to cut too wide a swath.

The manager must be a doer of things, a worker. The opportunities he sees from his executive desk have no meaning unless they are buttressed by his activity. A man may have talent and knowledge and the wish to progress, but these are futile unless he has driving power.

AN OPEN MIND

The manager needs not only an open-door policy but an open mind. This is not something that is picked up the day you are promoted; it has to be cultivated previously.

Tolerance distinguishes between what is essential and what is not. It enables you to extend your knowledge over great stretches of life so that you are better able to understand the small part that falls within your jurisdiction.

When a man has managerial responsibilities he must not allow himself to be diverted by side issues, however attractive they may be to him. This quality should be cultivated on the way up to avoid being sidetracked by things of no consequence in your program.

Single-minded ambition should not be allowed to deprive you of the color, flavor, poetry, passion, and the infinite variety of life. Even the most hardheaded managers need philosophy, art, literature, and ethics in order to be human. Philosophy is not an ivory tower diversion. It is a penetration to the principles and meanings of things, and these are of preeminent value to a manager.

ON REACHING MATURITY

A man's emotional maturity determines his ability to work effectively with other people. There is no credit due you for being old in years; that just happens. But to be mature in thinking is a credit to you because you have worked toward it and developed it. Maturity is a state of mind, not a date on a calendar.

Not all men are so eminently qualified that they can reach the top of the managerial tree. But anyone can rise to a better job in which he will be making the most of his talents. The path is never an unbroken series of successes, there will be disappointments and reverses that must be met staunchly.

The way to win success was put as clearly as need be by a little boy. When he was asked how he learned to skate he replied: "Oh, by getting up every time I fell down."

A good manager is one who isn't worried about his own career but rather the careers of those who work for him. My advice: don't worry about yourself; take care of those who work for you and you'll float to greatness on their achievements.

—H. S. M. BURNS

USE ALL OF YOUR ABILITY

by Philip Marvin

Dean of Professional Development,
University of Cincinnati

Only a few are sensitive to the fact that achieving success calls for much more than just doing a good job.

Most men find that they fall far short of being where they want to be at any particular time. Then, too, they find that they aren't making full use of their capabilities. Literally surrounded by unused abilities, they watch others moving ahead faster. Faced with this frustrating situation, they ask themselves, "Why?"

For the most part, the problem lies in the fact that men are trained to perform specialized functions but are not trained to make effective use of their talents. The man who takes time to develop the best way of doing his job, based on what has worked best in the past, often fails to apply the same analytical approach to get him where he wants to go. Moreover, most men don't know where they want to go until someone gets there first.

A few men develop sensitivity to the basic factors of high-level performance and reshape their attack on the future. Some of them search out the sources of success tapped by those who have moved forward most rapidly and formulate guidelines for others to follow. Here are the ten basic factors found to be common to high-level performers.

1. Learning from experience. High-level performers make good use of the experience of the past. As one man put it: "I don't have time to rediscover what's already known. Why repeat the mistakes others have made when you can follow in the footsteps of men who have proved that the way they do things has the best track record for successful achievement? Men who can't learn from experience waste a lot of time in every activity they undertake."

2. Action-oriented thinking. A second characteristic of the high-level performer is a determination to do things rather than to talk about them. He's a man who says, "I want to be where the action is. I like to be with people who do things. My greatest fear is that I'll miss out on some opportunities." The high-level performer has already done the job others are still talking about.

The action-oriented man is characteristically: searching out opportunities for action all of the time; afraid of acting too late; looking for ways to circumvent failure; actively exploring alternative courses of action; willing to take risks; determined to see jobs through; repeating patterns of action that have proved productive for himself and others in the past.

3. Detecting opportunities early. The man who says, "I'm waiting for someone to tip me off to something good," will probably wait a long time. The odds are poor. While he is waiting for someone to tell him about a good thing, the man spending his time searching out opportunities will move in and capitalize on the good opportunities.

The important thing isn't to wait until opportunity knocks; it's to know the sound when it's a mere tap.

The things that turn out to be good opportunities are like diamonds in the rough. Most people pass opportunities by because they aren't cut to size and don't sparkle like diamonds.

4. Sensitivity to lack of opportunity. One executive, in commenting on some decisions he had made in the course of his career, said, "A large part of my effectiveness has been due as much to things I didn't do as to things I did do. Most men lack a sixth sense that serves to warn them when they are wasting their time doing something that isn't worthwhile."

It's just as important to spot a lack of opportunity early as it is to spot opportunities. Times change. Men must change with the times.

It doesn't take any more effort to do worthwhile things than it does to perform routine jobs, but the long-run pay-off is greater when one spends time doing worthwhile things. Top performers are just as sensitive to situations offering little or no opportunity as they are to situations offering good opportunity. Above everything else, top performers avoid jobs having no future.

5. *Evaluation of potentials.* It's one thing to identify opportunities; it's another to be able to tie price tags to them so the most worthwhile opportunity can be selected.

In evaluating potentials, one must know one's own scale of values as well as the scale of others' values — balancing personal values against market values. A compromise may be necessary between a lower return when doing what one wants to do and a higher return when doing what others want.

6. *Building plans around capabilities.* Top performers concentrate their efforts on things they do well. Most men don't know which of their skills give them the best competitive advantage. As a result, they are often engaged in activities where they are wasting energy dog-paddling while competitors are conserving energy with a championship crawl stroke.

When a man knows his capabilities, he is in the best position to develop them effectively. One who is outstanding in one or two specialties is in a much stronger position than the man who maintains a position of mediocrity in many areas of specialization.

7. *Aiming at objectives.* Objectives distinguish effective action from aimless action. A man can't know what he's aiming at or how good his aim is without setting up targets.

Well-defined targets tell a man what not to shoot at too. Poor performers often earn their reputation by doing things that weren't needed or wanted. When poor performance is the result of poorly defined objectives, remedial steps can turn poor performers into productive men.

8. *Concentrating on effective effort.* There's a lot of difference between busyness, hard work, and effective effort.

Top performers rarely seem to be busy or exhausted from hard work. Low-level performers are among the busiest of men. As one executive put it, "I like men who know when to go home because the job is done. These are the men who know when to stay because the job isn't done." Too many men seem to think they are hired to work from eight to five. They miss the whole point of their value to the organization. Premiums are placed on effectiveness, not on efforts.

9. *Moving in and out of situations.* "I want men who are looking for better opportunities and who want to make a move to places where the opportunities are bigger and better. They're the best performers. These men want to show what they can do. I don't want men who are 'holing in' in safe spots and who are afraid to take risks."

Mobility must be a basic ingredient in any kind of effective action. High-level performers move into situations where they feel they can make a contribution and move out when they sense that they can no longer do anything worthwhile.

Top-level performers are aggressive. When the working climate isn't conducive to productive output, they initiate moves themselves. Low-level producers, on the other hand, act defensively. It's when somebody else decides that productivity must be stepped up that they see the handwriting on the wall and decide that they had better move before it's too late.

10. *Planning and controlling programs.* "I don't know of anyone who is more interested in a man's future than the man himself. I look for men who have set goals for their careers and have worked out a plan to get them where they want to go."

Top performers want to be in the driver's seat when it comes to controlling their destiny. They seek the counsel of men of experience on many matters; they plan their action, using guidelines based on experience; but they control their personal programs, recognizing that no one else has as great a stake in their future.

5

The Man and His Money

MONEY AND MEANING

by Wallace Denton

Associate Professor of Family Life, Purdue University

Money! The word rings in our minds like the bell on a cash register. However, because money is one of the top battlegrounds for marital quarrels, it may be that the bell is the one kept at ringside signaling time for another round in the marital bout. Whichever bell it is, its sound triggers various emotional reactions in the American breast.

The term "battleground" was used calculatedly. That is, the money quarrels unhappy couples bring to marriage counselors are infrequently the real problems. Rather, money is simply the battleground over which they fight about unspoken, and sometimes unconscious, deeper-lying issues.

Marriage counselors have noted that there is often a connection between the kind of conflicts a couple has and the way the partners handle their money. The behavior patterns of each partner tend to be reflected in the way each copes with money. Thus, for example, it is not uncommon to find that conflicts over impulse spending reflect a tendency on the part of one or both mates in other ways to impulsively "want what they want" without working together as a team.

An examination of marital money quarrels usually reveals that money as a battleground is a safer area on which to vent hostilities than the deeper-lying issues. Money is a more socially and emotionally acceptable area on which to display the stored-up resentments than if the real issues were faced openly and honestly.

One characteristic of life is that our possessions tend to take on secondary or symbolic meanings. An automobile is basically a means of transporting ourselves from one place to another. But an automobile from earliest times has developed other symbolic meanings. It symbolizes success, prestige, freedom, independence, even masculinity. Vance Packard in *The Hidden Persuaders* notes that a convertible is a mistress symbol to men.

Just as an automobile or clothes develop secondary meanings, even so does our money develop other meanings. Let's discuss some of the common attitudes that husbands and wives have toward money and how these manifest themselves in the family.

1. The first attitude is the "bathroom towel" attitude — His and Hers. This attitude occurs in families in which both the husband and the wife are employed and one or both insist on keeping the money they earn separate from the other. This practice has some inherent risks.

It is difficult to know whether separate bank accounts are a reflection or a cause of a lack of "we-ness" in a family. In any case, money is such a powerful symbol in our society that it is probably difficult for most couples to handle separate accounts skillfully. Separate accounts tend to contribute to a "my money" and "your money" attitude in the home instead of "our money." Unless a couple has good reason for it, it is doubtful that the risks of separate accounts are worth the advantages.

2. A second approach to money is the "I'll pick up the check" attitude. You can always count on this person picking up the check. He will even make a scene over the matter. This exhibitionistic spender has a need to impress others with his affluence, or his generosity. More important, he has a need to bolster his own ego, to reassure himself of his importance and success.

Mr. and Mrs. "I'll pick up the check" surround themselves with expensive "adult toys," such as boats, stereo record players, cameras, tape recorders, flashy cars, color televisions, and clothes with "proper" (i.e., prestigious) labels attached.

This kind of ostentation is one of the major motivations to which advertisers appeal. And it always works with Mr. and Mrs. "I'll pick up the check."

3. The "commanding general" attitude is held by those who view money as the key to controling others. It becomes a way of asserting, affirming, and commanding dominance and control over others — perhaps the wife.

Guy Smithers was such a husband. Mrs. Smithers had no idea how much money her husband made. He deposited a fixed amount in her checking account each month, out of which she paid the household bills. Furthermore, he carefully scrutinized the monthly balance sheet from the bank and expected her to account for any money spent on nonroutine items. She complained of feeling treated as a child on an allowance. Mrs. Smithers was extremely unhappy, but felt that her husband's control over the finances made it difficult for her to do much about it.

The "commanding general" also uses his money to bestow favors upon those who are submissive to his dominance.

Counselors working in university settings often see students whose families continue to use the checkbook to exercise control over their single or married children. The parents of one married student even continued sending a monthly check after their son had told his parents that he and his wife could live without it. This economic dependence is often enough to squelch any signs of independence on the part of a son or daughter. Fortunately, in this case, the son thereafter returned the monthly checks — much to the parents' consternation. You see, they needed to give him money. Without it, Mr. "Commanding General" had no more control over his son.

4. "Here's a dollar's worth of love" attitude is found in those families where one or both partners think love, like

other things in their lives, can be purchased for the price of the dollar.

Bill Elsworth was a rather rigid, undemonstrative man who seemed to have difficulty establishing or tolerating close, intimate relationships. Patty, his wife, complained that he rarely seemed to take a personal interest in her or express any feelings of love — unless he was interested in sex. Yet, Bill rather regularly brought Patty gifts of jewelry, clothes, and perfumes. When in a quarrel she complained that their house was an emotional desert, he became angry and reminded her of the gifts. "I notice you haven't turned down any of my gifts," he said accusingly. "But don't you see," she responded, "I want you, not your gifts." These ideas are incomprehensible to men such as Bill Elsworth.

Mr. "Dollar's worth of love" is a person who is also likely to spend little time with his children. He is making money. He is busy "getting to the top."

He seems to see himself as having nothing worth bestowing on his family except another dollar. Illness, retirement, or loss of his job hit him especially hard, for they strike at his most critical point — his ability to earn a dollar. Since he tends to see all things as being measured by the value of a dollar, and since his own identity is so closely tied to the dollar mark, he feels useless and worthless. No longer can he offer a "dollar's worth of love." He has nothing to offer.

5. The "save for a rainy day" attitude is held by those who live under the constant fear of impending financial doom — the loss of a job, economic depression, illness, or accident. Consequently, these people oversave.

For example, Helen Rice grew up during the years of the Great Depression. More than thirty years later she recalls with great vividness her ragged clothes, the toyless Christmases, and her father's crying over the family's poverty. She lives in fear of another similar occurrence. She constantly hounds her husband to save more money even though they have a year's salary in savings. Of course, this is considerably more than the reserves usually recommended for a family.

6. Related to the above is the "pack rat" attitude toward money. This person does not seem to be reacting to any particular past deprivation, nor is he saving for anything in particular. Mr. "Pack rat" simply enjoys collecting money. To get a "pack rat" to spend his money sometimes makes him almost paranoid. He may assume that everyone, including (or especially) his wife, is trying to get his money.

7. On the opposite end of the continuum is the "Don't save it for your kids to fight over" attitude. Rather than oversaving, this person overspends.

The overspender is often trying to compensate for past deprivations. Some who grow up in destitute circumstances seem bent on a frenzied attempt to make up for all their past privations and buy all the things they feel they missed as children. This leads them deeper and deeper into debt as they pursue their impulses for the trinkets of an affluent society. "Buy now, pay later" is the gospel of modern high-pressure salesmanship.

Unfortunately what Mr. and Mrs. "Don't save it for your kids to fight over" confront is that they may not have enough for the children *now* when they make their many monthly payments.

8. The "bull whip" attitude toward money is the final one to be considered here. In this case, money is viewed as a weapon to crack over the heads of recalcitrant family members. Anyone who fails to fall into line is whipped into submission, with money used as the whip.

A wife who withholds sexually (her weapon) may find Mr. "Bull whip" retaliating by withholding money from her. Children who are disobedient have their allowances withheld by Mr. and Mrs. "Bull whip." One of the main reasons why family specialists usually advise against cutting allowances as punishment is that this tends to put a dollar value on conforming behavior. The parent may unwittingly communicate to the child that money and love are tied up together. "When you obey me, I love you more; I give you your money," may be what the child perceives the parent as saying.

Money, like fire, is a faithful servant but a tyrannical master. Because of this, we must either master our money or be forever intimidated and dominated by it. But making peace with money is not easy. Some suggestions might be of help.

The first law of finance is that a person must live within his income. Many families that make twice the national average have more problems than families that make half the national average. How can this be? The answer lies mainly in the attitudes that people have toward money, and one of the main economic "sins" is to spend more than one makes.

Family finances require family cooperation. The family's spending pattern must command everyone's loyalty and, therefore, must satisfy every family member as being fair. If the plan is to be workable, the planning should be done by the family, not by one individual.

If you are in financial straits, perform an "autopsy" on your spending habits. Careful examination of where your money goes will sometimes reveal places where cuts and savings can be made. It is not enough to blame inflation, bad luck, sickness, or circumstances. Something must be done to bring outlay more into line with income.

Finally, let the mate who is most adept at the task handle the money. Some men have an idea that the prime responsibility for the family budget must be theirs — if they are really men. However, I am not aware of anything written in the laws of nature that says a man ought to handle the family finances. The reality of the situation is that the wife may be the person who is best equipped temperamentally and otherwise to handle money.

"The love of money is the root of all evil," one New Testament writer asserted (1 Timothy 6:10). We cannot avoid facing the fact that unhealthy and immature attitudes toward money are at the base of many family difficulties.

INVITATION TO PROSPERITY

by Charles Blair

Pastor, Calvary Temple, Denver

Why is it that man instinctively wants to prosper? I believe this urge is part of our "likeness and image of God." It is God's nature to be prosperous, so it is our nature to want to attain prosperity.

Prosperity is a divine idea. The devil knows only how to pervert and destroy prosperity. God is the author of prosperity; Satan, of the "poverty program." Poverty is part of the curse of sin. There will come a time when Satan will be bound, and poverty and misery will be replaced by peace and prosperity.

To begin, we need to have the proper perspective on prosperity.

PERSPECTIVE ON PROSPERITY

As we scan the Bible, there emerges the certainty that a prosperous God wants his children to be prosperous. "Let the Lord be magnified, which hath pleasure in the prosperity of his servant" (Psalm 35:27). "Both riches and honor come from thee" (1 Chronicles 29:12). "And his (Joseph's) master (Potiphar) saw that the Lord was with him and that the Lord made all he did to prosper" (Genesis 39:3).

In the parable of the talents, Jesus praised the servants who invested and multiplied their original investments. He condemned the servant who hid his talent and made no effort to increase it. Jesus never condemned riches; he condemned the rich for failing to obey God's laws.

If God's law of prosperity is to operate in our lives, we must believe that it is God's will for us to prosper. "But without faith it is impossible to please him" (Hebrews 11:6).

APPROPRIATING PROSPERITY

Appropriating prosperity requires an active faith in a living God. Let the roots of your faith sink deep into the promises of God. We can compare this faith with the confidence that we express in a reliable mail order company. We select the items we want from the catalog, place an order, and in a few days receive a confirmation stating that the items will be mailed within a certain number of days. Then we look forward to arrival.

"And if we know that he hears us, whatsoever we ask, we know that we have the petitions that we desired of him" (1 John 5:15).

The writer of Deuteronomy says, "But thou shalt remember the Lord thy God; for it is he that giveth thee power to get wealth."

God is not only the source of power, but he gives his children power to become successful. Is God interested in the world of business? Even some Christians doubt that he is concerned with their bank accounts or material assets. However, the testimony of God's Word clearly states: "I am the Lord thy God which teacheth thee to profit, which leadeth thee by the way that thou shouldest go" (Isaiah 48:17).

For this reason, I suggest that you invite God into your business and be partners in prosperity.

PARTNERS IN PROSPERITY

And when you consider that God is the source of any ability or wealth that you may have, it only makes sense to hand the controls over to him. It makes good business sense to make him the senior partner, since he is the more qualified one to be the head of the business.

Yes, God cares about you and your business, and this interest is born out of the loving heart of a father who would see us prosper. He wants to teach us to prosper.

What reassurance — to know that the omnipotent, omniscient God stands ready to take the helm of our lives and share this wisdom with us. God — who has all knowledge and wisdom — sees around the bend in the road. From his lofty position he knows what is impossible for me to know.

DIVINE DIRECTION

"In all thy ways acknowledge him and he shall direct thy paths" (Proverbs 3:6). It is ours to acknowledge and God's to direct. But continuous direction requires continuous acknowledgment. If we want guidance in all our ways, we must acknowledge him in all our ways.

No man has ever failed who waited until he heard God's voice and then followed. Study the life of faithful, trusting Joseph and you will be convinced that God wants to direct every detail of your life.

PRINCIPLES OF PROSPERITY

You can't trample on the rights and feelings of others, charge high prices for shoddy merchandise, and at the same time expect God to bless your business. The Apostle Paul says, "Provide things honest in the sight of all men." We need to be men of integrity whether it be in advertising, on the income tax return, or in business and social relationships.

Obeying the Golden Rule is fundamental to godly prosperity. "All things whatsoever ye would that men should do to you, do ye even so to them" (Matthew 7:12).

The Christian is charitable, humble, forgiving. He takes to heart the words of Paul: "Bless them which persecute you: bless, and curse not. Rejoice with them that do rejoice, and weep with them that weep" (Romans 12:15).

Can you love a competitor, especially one who makes life difficult for you? Yes, you can pray for him, and God will fill your heart with good will toward that man.

Then there's diligence. Being a Christian businessman is a full-time job. It requires hard work, sacrifice, and service. But if one follows the rules of prosperity, prosperity will follow.

Having a specific goal to work toward concentrates effort

and serves as a means of evaluation. Paul set a definite goal: "This one thing I do, forgetting those things which are behind, and reaching forth unto those things which are before, I press toward the mark for the prize of the high calling of God in Christ Jesus" (Philippians 3:13, 14).

GOD-GIVEN GOALS

The Christian who is in partnership with God is setting God-given goals. This requires much prayer. Someone may say: I don't have time to pray or to play. I just plunge and believe God will help me." This is neither divine guidance nor common sense. Jesus said, "For which of you, intending to build a tower, sitteth not down first, and counteth the cost, whether he have sufficient to finish it? Lest haply after he hath laid a foundation, and is not able to finish it, all that behold it begin to mock him" (Luke 14: 28-30).

Yes, God may lead you into a business venture which requires a great deal of faith, but be sure it is God's leading and not just your enthusiasm.

PRIORITIES

Material success must not be an end in itself. As Christians, our primary purpose is to glorify the heavenly Father, and this requires putting God and his kingdom first. Materialistic priorities will terminate at the grave, whereas laying up treasures in heaven will pay eternal dividends.

God's interests must always be first. Advancing the kingdom of God takes priority; business and personal interests are secondary.

Proper priorities will automatically lead to divine dividends.

DIVINE DIVIDENDS

"Give, and it shall be given to you; good measure, pressed down, and shaken together, and running over, shall men give into your bosom" (Luke 6:38).

Here is a law of the Kingdom of God: Christlike giving

does bring abundant returns. We simply cannot outgive God. This giving-receiving principle is a continuous cycle. Recognizing this, the Apostle Paul encouraged his fellow Christians to be generous. "He which soweth sparingly shall reap also sparingly, and he which soweth bountifully shall reap also bountifully" (2 Corinthians 9:6).

In view of the fact that tithing was instituted seven hundred years before the Law was given, Christians continue to tithe, but it is rather difficult for me to believe that the New Testament Church gave only the tithe. They were to give proportionately in ratio to their income. "Upon the first day of the week let every one of you lay by him in store as God hath prospered him" (1 Corinthians 16:2).

Christ taught a gospel that is not restricted by law; it goes "the second mile," it gives liberally and cheerfully. If our giving is motivated by love, then the legalistic tithe will not be enough to satisfy our desire to give to our Master. Prove God now!

Tithing is minimum giving. Tithing is legalistic giving and can often be done grudgingly, but God wants you to enjoy high-level giving — "spontaneous giving." He wants you to have prosperity-plus.

Why not put a ceiling on our own standard of living and take the lid off to spontaneous, love-motivated giving!

A well-balanced conception of prosperity includes stewardship. Every Christian knows that he is not his own, that he is God-created and blood-bought. Everything he is and has is the Lord's. It is God's money that he handles, and "It is required in stewards that a man be found faithful" (1 Corinthians 4:2). God has set a high premium on faithfulness.

RESPONSIBLE PROSPERITY

A steward must be faithful in the use of his time and talents. Each of us has the same amount of time at our disposal. You don't "find" time for God; you "take" the time.

Be willing to give your time, your services, and your

money. I do not believe that God blesses us with prosperity so that we may heap to ourselves increasing luxuries. He gives us prosperity so that we may use it to bless mankind. One day our Lord shall return and we shall all stand before him to give an account of our stewardship. God grant that we shall all hear the words, "Well done, thou good and faithful servant" (Matthew 25:21).

You will never stub your toe standing still. The faster you go, the more chance there is of stubbing your toe, but the more chance you have of getting somewhere.

—CHARLES F. KETTERING

DON'T DROWN IN DEBT

The Morans are fast approaching a financial crisis. Over the past two years they have acquired a new car, a washing machine, and a color television, all on time. They have run up a $500 balance in their revolving charge accounts, which they are paying off at the rate of 10 percent a month. A little while ago they borrowed a few hundred dollars from a small-loan company to clear up overdue medical bills.

All in all, the Morans owe $2,800 in short-term debt. The payments are draining $175 a month from a take-home pay of $700. That leaves $525 to support a family of four. They have managed to keep afloat so far only by scrimping on necessities. The frills — vacations, occasional meals out, parties, and so on — went long ago. They are so short of cash that as fast as they pay down a revolving charge account, they have to add new purchases to the balance. When they finish paying a small-loan company, they will have to borrow again for the youngsters' dental work.

Their only buffer against an emergency is a carefully conserved $200 savings account.

How do families like the Morans get into such a fix? Sometimes they are plunged into financial trouble by the sudden loss of a job, a severe illness, or other misfortune. But often they simply slide into debt, which is easy enough to do. If your credit rating is good or fair, you can buy just about anything you want on time, from a vacation to a college education. You can overload yourself with debt even if your credit record is bad. Lenders aren't likely to object to your buying on time — until you stop paying on time.

These signals mean danger

Hardly any family needs to founder in debt without knowing what's going on. The signs of credit trouble are unmistakable and as clear as flashing red lights. Here are five of the easiest warnings to spot:

Reprinted by permission from *Changing Times,* the Kiplinger Magazine (February 1969 issue). Copyright 1969 by The Kiplinger Washington Editors, Inc., 1729 H Street, N.W., Washington, D.C.

156 /

A substantial share — 20 percent or more — of your take-home pay goes to cover debt payments. By any measure, one dollar out of every five you get is a lot to devote to debt. The average family's debt payment is 14 percent of income. The Moran's debt-payment level was up to 25 percent.

You have been stretching out your debts by borrowing for longer and longer periods. True, you can reduce your monthly installments that way. But you increase the cost of your debt and make yourself more vulnerable to an unforeseen loss of income or an emergency. In a sense, you're betting you won't need the money now going to your creditors for not just six months, say, but for a year or perhaps longer.

You let your debts snowball by adding new obligations before paying off old ones. There's nothing inherently wrong with having more than one debt outstanding, provided you keep the total within bounds. One safety rule you can set is never to owe more at any one time than you can repay within twelve months at your current rate of payments. Say you are paying $100 a month — regularly, not just one month — on debts totaling $3,000. In twelve months you will have repaid only $1,200. You would have to increase your payments to $250 a month to stay within the twelve-month limit. If you can't afford $250 a month, this rule would warn you that you can't afford $3,000 of debt. It would have warned the Morans, for it will take them about a year and five months to pay their creditors.

This particular guideline cannot be applied, of course, to home loans, home-modernization loans, college loans, and other very large loans that, because of their size and the long-term value of what they buy, usually are written for longer terms.

You always have outstanding debts with banks or lending companies. You may be taking out a new loan as soon as an old one is paid off (as the Morans intend to do), or you may be using the proceeds of a new loan to pay an old one.

Either way, you're on a credit treadmill, always in debt and always paying interest.

You are frequently delinquent on payments and can't seem to catch up. This is one symptom that should never be ignored. If you can't handle your present debts, how in the world can you shoulder any new ones?

Find your personal debt limit

Naturally, you want to quit on credit well before those danger signals start flashing. Probably you know from experience how much you can afford to spend on food, clothing, housing, and other living costs. Budgeting for debt requires a little more planning because you have to find a realistic debt limit geared to your particular financial situation and needs. It must, at the same time, leave you a prudent margin of safety so that you can make payments without undue pain.

The family debt form has been devised to help you develop a personal debt limit by following the four steps described below. The process rests on the principle that there is a reciprocal relationship between debt and what you can spend for other purposes. Every debt contracted spends part of your future income that would otherwise be available for living expenses and savings.

Here is how to calculate your debt limit:

1. Start with your take-home pay and add any steady outside income you may have — interest on savings accounts, dividends and the like. Don't include any income, such as overtime and bonuses, that you can't depend on regularly. Debt payments, remember, are almost always fixed obligations; you can't change them from month to month to accommodate changes in your income.

2. List all your monthly living costs in the "actual" expense column, the fixed ones exactly and the variable ones as closely as your records and experience will allow.

3. Next, the most crucial step. Review each expense category and eliminate any extras that you could *easily* do without. Husbands and wives should work this out together;

better to compromise now than to battle later. You won't be able to squeeze much out of essentials, so concentrate on the discretionary items. Notice that the form has a line for savings and investments. If you have already accumulated an adequate savings fund for emergencies (equal to at least half a year's take-home pay), you may be prepared to cut back there. But try not to eliminate long-term savings programs for, say, buying a home or education.

List your new, trimmed-down budget — including any amounts you prefer not to change — in the "reduced" expenses column.

4. Deduct total reduced expenses from the total income figure. The difference represents the *maximum* you can afford each month for debt payments.

If you want to use the twelve-month rule of thumb mentioned earlier, the total amount of debt at any time should not exceed twelve times your monthly payment limit.

If you're expecting a nice pay raise in a few months, you will be tempted to add that to your limit to give yourself more leeway. That's risky. Don't do it unless you are as certain of getting the raise as you can be certain that the bank or store will want its payments whether you get the raise or not.

To check whether you are operating within a safe debt-payment limit, figure your present debt load in the bottom section of the form.

Now play it smart

Knowing your borrowing limit is only half the battle. The other half, equally important, is knowing how to borrow wisely. The prudent family does most of its buying out of current income or savings, borrowing only occasionally and only for worthwhile purposes. Above all, it does not become mesmerized by the idea that borrowing really is just "saving in reverse." That mischievous misconception forgets that you pay interest on borrowed money and, at the same time, lose the interest you might have earned had you saved up instead of borrowing.

For maximum mileage from your credit power, follow these common sense rules:

Credit is expensive, so don't borrow unless you must. The 1½ percent service charge on an ordinary revolving charge account is equivalent to 18 percent a year interest. A 6½ percent bank loan repaid in installments works out to about 13 percent a year because of the way the loan is set up.

Before you borrow or buy on time, use whatever free credit you can get. Probably you can cover such big items as television sets or a dryer with a regular thirty-day charge account. If you buy at the start of the billing cycle, you won't be billed for about thirty days, and then you have another thirty days to pay.

Don't tie yourself down to a long-term loan for small amounts or for things with a short life. If you finance a vacation on a two-year loan, you will still be paying on last year's vacation when next year's rolls around. On the other hand, it's reasonable to finance home improvements over a long period because you will continue to enjoy them as long as you live in the house. Moreover, you may recoup part of the cost when you sell.

Always shop around to check interest rates. You may find that it's cheaper to finance a car with a bank than with a dealer. And why use 18 percent store credit when you can borrow from a bank or your credit union for 13 percent or less?

You may be able to save, too, by negotiating a different kind of loan. A bank will sometimes lend to good clients on short term notes at a much lower rate than it charges for ordinary installment loans. Collateralized loans in which you pledge stock, real estate, a savings account, or some other asset as security are normally less expensive than unsecured loans.

Don't sign a loan contract until you make sure all the terms are clearly spelled out. Many families with credit problems never bothered to ask how much their loans cost. Are you playing debt brinkmanship like the Moran family? Do you see any warning symptoms in your financial situation? Are you spending more on debt payments than the debt limit allows? Are you careless about arranging credit, taking the first proposition that comes along?

If you have to answer yes to any of those questions, it's time to reform. If you can answer no to all, congratulations. You're in control of your credit; it's not in control of you.

FAMILY DEBT FORM

Enter your own figures to calculate a safe, practical monthly debt-payment limit for yourself. Use the bottom section to see how your present payments compare with that limit.

Monthly income

TAKE-HOME PAY	_____
OTHER INCOME	_____
TOTAL INCOME	_____

Monthly expenses	actual	reduced
FIXED:		
mortgage or rent	_____	_____
life insurance	_____	_____
house insurance	_____	_____
auto insurance	_____	_____
local taxes	_____	_____
VARIABLE:		
utilities	_____	_____
medical (including health insurance)	_____	_____
food	_____	_____
clothing	_____	_____
recreation	_____	_____
furnishings & other household expenses	_____	_____
savings, investments	_____	_____
other	_____	_____
total expenses	_____	_____

your monthly debt-payment limit: deduct reduced expenses from income _____

YOUR PRESENT DEBTS

Purpose of loan	Amount left to pay	Monthly installments
car	_____	_____
home-modernization loan	_____	_____
household equipment	_____	_____
charge accounts	_____	_____
other	_____	_____
total	_____	_____

No man can fight his way to the top and stay at the top without exercising the fullest measure of grit, courage, determination, resolution. Every man who gets anywhere does so because he has first firmly resolved to progress in the world and then has enough stick-to-it-tiveness to transform his resolution into reality. Without resolution, no man can win any worthwhile place among his fellowmen.

—B. C. FORBES

TEN WAYS TO GIVE SENSIBLY

by Robert F. Sharpe

Financial Consultant

Most people don't give sensibly. We may be canny and careful about earning, spending, and saving. But when it comes to giving, most of us are careless, thoughtless, impulsive, and sentimental.

Here are some of the foolish things we do:

We don't plan our giving; therefore, each request creates a "can I or not?" decision crisis.

We give according to our mood-of-the-moment; therefore, we invariably give either too much or too little.

We don't take the time and trouble to investigate; therefore, we often give to causes that are either unworthy or less worthy than they seem.

We don't know how to say no gracefully; therefore, we give token amounts to organizations we don't really want to help and then regret having done so.

We've never thought enough about how much we *should* give; therefore, we go around feeling guilty half the time about giving too little and laughably self-satisfied at other times over small gestures which we think confirm our "generosity."

We ignore many tax-saving opportunities in giving (perhaps because we feel that would shadow our giving motives); therefore, we overlook the fact that tax deductions make it possible for us to give *more*.

We overlook special channels of giving that can increase the impact and effectiveness of our gifts (such as annuities, trusts, revocable gifts.).

We overlook channels of giving that can, in many cases, *increase* our income and add to our personal and family security.

As one who had been involved for years in helping churches, denominations, mission boards, colleges, hospitals, and other non-profit organizations raise funds, I would like to suggest ten ways that each of us can give more sensibly.

1. Budget a total for the year. Just sit down and decide calmly how much you can afford to give over the next twelve months. Then categorize it — so much to the church, so much to the community's united fund, so much to any other types of worthy causes you wish to support. Allow a contingency fund as businessmen do for unforeseen emergencies. Include in it a certain amount for impulsive "fun giving" within sensible limits.

2. Investigate the requesting organization. Naturally, you would not knowingly give to an unworthy organization. But remember — there are types and degrees of worthiness. Happily, there are very few out-and-out swindlers hiding behind titles containing such popular words as "missions," "gospel," etc. But many worthy causes use too much of your gift for administrative or fund-raising purposes; the ratio can vary from 2 percent to 98 percent, and does. Then, there are worthy organizations who duplicate each other's work. Still others simply have poor leadership. There are also some organizations that don't need your help as badly as others. So don't hesitate to ask for full information. Read the literature provided. Check whether their work is as vital as others that seek your support.

3. Ask yourself, "Who will if I don't?" When you're deciding which organizations you will help and which you won't, it's good to ponder the question, "Who will help if I don't?" or "What will happen if I don't give and others don't either?"

Will the need be met anyway? Will the organization launch another campaign of another type? Will it have to cut back on essential activities? Will it have to go out of business? If it did, would other organizations do the work? Would foundations step in? Would the government?

People who complain about government expansionism should ask themselves if they've done all they could and should to meet those needs through private channels. Private philanthropy can be a formidable force for keeping the government out of problems that can be solved better through individual initiative. Someone has said, "If we had given more to missions in the early 1900s, we might have avoided World War II."

4. *Go ahead and say "No."* Once you have budgeted, investigated, and planned, you will be armed with facts that will make it much easier to say no to those you have to turn down. You can always say it regretfully, with a smile.

You can say: "I'm sorry, but I can only support my own church." Or: "I just can't give to all the medical causes, so I had to decide to support the few in which I'm especially interested." Or: "I'm sure your work is worthwhile, but I'm already supporting an organization that does similar work."

5. *Consider long-range needs separately.* Many worthy causes want to put themselves out of business as soon as possible by solving a pressing temporary problem or emergency. Others have needs for which there is no end in sight, and probably never will be. Will there ever be a day when churches, colleges, and mission boards don't require support? Such a thought is almost inconceivable. Our giving should reflect the fact that these organizations have long-range needs as well as immediate ones.

Most of us never even think of it, yet our "giving power" is much greater when it comes to long-range needs. It's greater, first, because we have more to give. We don't need to limit our giving to "this month's spare cash" or even this year's. We can think in terms of future gifts — insurance policies, real estate, securities, livestock, crops, business assets. Our giving power is greater, also, because there's time for the gift to grow.

6. *Make charitable bequests in your will.* I assume you *have* a will, although over half the adults in the U.S.A. don't. Remember you can extend your influence far into the future, far beyond the grave, by means of a bequest to a worthy organization. Remember, too, that *only* through a will can you do this. If you die without a will, the state will distribute your property only to nearest kin, and cannot,

of course, even consider any charitable causes you favor. Most people leave everything to their relatives without stopping to think, "Do they really need it?" If you can't do it wholly, consider naming the organization as a partial or remainder beneficiary of your estate.

7. *Take advantage of tax savings.* Recognize that the federal government not only subsidizes individual benevolence, but does it *deliberately* as a matter of policy and tradition. Built into the tax system is the encouragement of philanthropy. The thoughtful giver takes advantage of every possible such saving in order to give *more*. I believe personally that the giving motive is far stronger than the tax one; few people give merely to avoid taxes.

Keep in mind the crucial difference between "tax avoidance" and "tax evasion." If you detour to use a free bridge to avoid a toll bridge, that's tax avoidance — legal, smart, commendable. If you crash the gate to avoid paying, that's tax evasion — illegal. Don't evade, but do avoid taxes when possible and enhance your giving potential. The government encourages tax avoidance so long as it is legal.

Many people fear that tax reform will change this basic stance. It has not to date. In fact, tax reforms have strengthened it.

Recent tax reform made it possible to increase the amount of deducted gifts to approved nonprofit organizations. The percentage was increased from 30 percent to 50 percent of adjusted gross income.

If you give in one year more than 50 percent of that year's income, you can still use the carry-over privilege to deduct the excess over future years, i.e., this year and the five succeeding tax years.

The standard deduction (if one chooses not to itemize his deductions), 10 percent of adjusted gross income with a maximum of $1,000, has now been increased to $2,000.

You can give appreciated property such as stocks, bonds, and real estate and deduct the gift at fair market value (but here the 30-percent limit applies to deductions, unless you first report any capital gains that would have been realized on a sale.)

8. *Consider property gifts.* Many people who feel they "can't afford to give" are thinking solely in terms of cash. Truly, they can't afford to give cash because they have so little, but can well afford to give certain types of property. In fact, gifts of property (stocks, bonds, real estate, etc.) can often rescue people from a tax bind and add to current cash income. So consider giving property, and explore the possibilities of such gifts. You may be pleasantly surprised.

9. *Consider revocable gifts.* Many organizations actively seek revocable gifts — the kind you can take back in case of emergency. It may seem fickle, but it's actually quite sensible for both donor and recipient. The donor has the security of knowing he can revoke the gift if he has to and the recipient has the comforting knowledge that very few donors actually do revoke their gifts, while most are able to give much more generously than they would otherwise due to the protective feature. The gift becomes definite at death, but passes directly to the receiving organization, without being subject to estate tax or probate costs or delays.

10. *Consider giving for income.* No, that's not a typographical error. While most people give *from* income, some give *for* additional income, actually increasing their income by means of judicious giving. This apparent "magic" is usually brought about by converting idle property into income and taking tax benefits which sometimes "free up" additional income. The details need not be discussed here. You get them from the planned giving officer of the organization you want to help or from your attorney, certified public accountant, bank trust officer, life insurance agent, or securities specialist.

So much for the ten "hows" of giving more sensibly; the why should go without saying: because it is our responsibility as Christians and as citizens.

Thomas Jefferson put it well: "Every man has two duties to charity — to devote a certain portion of his income for charitable purposes, and to see it so applied as to do the most good of which it is capable."

Since "God loveth a cheerful giver," we can surely assume that he cherishes even more the smiling, generous donor who is also inquisitive, informed, judicious, careful — in a word, *sensible.*

(*Because this article contains information on taxes that may change without notice, you are cautioned to check any statements that concern you with your own trusted tax advisor. This material is available for reprint and distribution by your church or other nonprofit organization. For complete information, write to Robert F. Sharpe & Co., Inc., Clark Tower, 5050 Poplar Avenue, Memphis, Tennessee, 38117.*)

> *J. B. Gambrell said, "It is not thinkable from the standpoint of the cross that anyone would give less under grace than the Jews gave under law."*
>
> *It has been said of the tithe that Abraham commenced it, Jacob continued it, Moses confirmed it, Malachi commanded it, and Christ commended it.*

—KNIGHT'S ILLUSTRATIONS FOR TODAY

BUILDING AN ESTATE

from Royal Bank of Canada Monthly Letter

A few people have the shortsighted and selfish attitude that they should enjoy what they earn by spending here and now. Most people are not spendthrifts like that. They know that pleasure enjoyed at the expense of their own or another's pain is not something to delight in. But not all of them know how to go about striking a balance between immediate enjoyment and future comfort.

The secret is to build an estate. Everyone has an estate of some sort, even if it consists only of the clothes he wears, but the estate that counts toward happiness and security and serenity is the one deliberately set up and developed.

The worry may not show itself, but every man is aware subconsciously of a yearning toward a feeling of financial security, and though they may stifle the signs of it, wives and children who are in the dark about the future live under a cloud of foreboding.

While a man lives, he shares with his family the advantages of his life. Upon his death, these advantages are replaced in part by a monetary benefit he has had the foresight to provide.

In its sentimental aspect, a human life may be altogether priceless, but there is no denying that there are hard financial facts to be faced. When the breadwinner is taken out of the picture, his income stops but the needs of his family continue.

The emotional upset caused by death is terrible and the loss of affection irreparable, but the fact cannot be ignored that life must go on for those who are left. How free it is from hardship will have been decided in large part by the provision made by the affectionate breadwinner.

He will have gone about this in a businesslike way, estimating the need, accumulating and conserving his resources, investing intelligently, and using all the other facilities which the modern economic and social structure has to offer for meeting the emergencies arising out of the uncertainties of life.

Doing this has a bonus value in that it makes his lifetime more secure and his retirement more free from worry.

We must fail in any attempt to estimate the value of a man to his family on the basis of affection and the psychological satisfaction derived from the fact of living together as a family, but his money value is a real, tangible thing.

Your money value, based upon your earning power, provides a rational basis for planning your estate so as to meet the responsibilities you owe to yourself and to your family.

A FAMILY PARTNERSHIP

The family should be regarded as a business partnership in addition to the values it has socially. It should learn about the facts of economic life so as to be able to manage money matters with a minimum of anxiety. The perplexity which faces a woman whose husband has just died may be lightened by his thoughtful arrangement of his estate during his lifetime.

Some men neglect to take their wives into the secret of managing finances. They labor under the delusion that the hand that rocks the cradle will not appear so appealing and charming if it helps him to count the cash income and the outgo. That is not a reasonable attitude. Every man is aware of his own desire to know about his future; let him think, then, of his wife's even more imperative need to know where she stands.

A man sometimes finds it hard to keep his financial balance; how, then, unless he allows her to participate in handling family finances, is his wife to learn how to do it on her own? The days of widowhood are strange, mournful, and difficult days which may be made easier if the family has been shown the financial foundation built for them and instructed in how to erect a new way of life on it.

Some men, fewer now than a couple of generations ago, are so situated that they cannot hope to do more than provide their families with a decent living, carry enough life insurance to tide over a transition period, and build up a small savings account. But even a moderate income, if wisely managed, will provide something for the future.

AN ESTATE

Building an estate does not involve higher mathematics or use of a slide rule. It can be done with the aid of simple arithmetic plus a determination to sort out the things that matter and give them priority.

Your first task is to find out as nearly as you can exactly where you are now and how far it is to where you want to go. Check the facts as they are today, weigh your responsibilities, estimate the factors you can control in some measure, take account of factors you cannot control, forecast needs, and plot a course.

A good planning chart will have three divisions: what you own; what you owe; reconciliation. The first will list real estate, furniture, savings, stocks, automobile, and other property; the second will cover amounts owing on mortgage, car, other installment purchases, and loans; the third will tabulate what life insurance policies, social security benefits, savings, retirement benefits and all other assets are needed and can be acquired to bring the first and second columns into balance.

Another method is to make a triple list covering the present time, the time of retirement, and the time when you are no longer there to manage things.

List every expense under such main headings as: shelter, food, transportation, vacation, income tax, charitable donations, church contributions, life and other personal insurance premiums, gifts.

You will have three columns. Under "present" you will list the amounts currently expended; under "retirement" leave out the items which will not apply (like travel to business, lunches); under "estate" leave out the items which do not apply (e.g. life insurance) and reduce those for which the cost will be lower (vacation, laundry, medical). The result will be a realistic three-sided picture of your money value and the demands upon it.

Some persons may feel that making an estimate of this kind is too troublesome, but the fact is that it is a trouble-saver and a mind-saver.

The more complete your plan is to start with, the easier it will be to operate and the fewer adjustments you will have to make in it. Also, and this is important, the planning you do now for your own and your family's future is the expression of your personality.

ON MAKING A WILL

To dispose of our property in the way we wish is one of the privileges of the democratic way of life. We should not reject this freedom by leaving the job to an austere government department.

Your will is the instrument by which you express your well-considered wishes regarding distribution of your property. To shrink from will-making is to endanger the comfort and the well-being of your family.

This era prides itself on facing realities starkly, but there is one reality some people refuse to look at — that of death. Emotions become mixed up with practicalities.

Vital persons face facts and plan their goals. They take all the measures necessary to influence and ensure the fulfilment of their aims and desires. They know that a will is a necessary and unique instrument. When it takes effect they will no longer be on hand to give testimony or explain their desires.

What they want to do in the way of giving protection and care to their families must be clearly set forth in the will so as to satisfy legal requirements.

No generalization can be made about making a will except one: everybody should make one. An extreme example is given in *Changing Times,* the Kiplinger Magazine. Suppose you had no money put aside and lived in a furnished apartment with only your clothes to call your own. Suppose that the bus on which you rode to work one morning was in an accident in which you were killed. Someone — your widow, mother, children, sister — should be able to collect enough damages from the negligent party to at least pay your funeral expenses. But if you left no will naming a beneficiary and an executor there would be difficulty in establishing a legal right to put in a claim.

Consider a more common occurrence: a man who owns real estate dies without making a will. His widow will be greatly hampered. She cannot sell the real estate to support herself and her children without an order from a court.

Some people think that the settlement of an estate is more expensive under a will than when there is none. The reverse is almost always true. The lawyer, notary, or other expert who draws up your will is aware of the ways in which to conserve money. There are exemptions from succession duties of which to take advantage: for children; certain gift bequests; property bequeathed for religious, charitable, or educational purposes; and others.

BUILDING AN ESTATE

When you start building an estate for your future years or for your family you need to be first of all a realist. Things are not always what they seem. For example, your *real* income is far below the dollar amount opposite your name in the payroll record. The cost of living index enables you to get a closer approximation of your purchasing power, because real income means the sum of the things you can buy with your money.

Besides the *level* of living, which is largely determined by the cost of things, you need to pay attention to the *standard* of living. This is not merely a matter of maintaining life through providing shelter, food, and clothing; it has also something to do with social customs and individual tastes.

Things which were looked upon only a few years ago as rare luxuries are now regarded as essential to comfort and self-respect, and combine with the essentials to make up a standard of living. The ordinary home has comforts which were not available even to kings a century ago. The only sure way of providing that this standard shall be maintained now and in the future is by planning. It is a matter of combining mature common sense, experience, power of will, and a few principles.

There is no budget that will suit every family. Statistics that give the average amount spent on this and that are useful only to statisticians. Your family is a unique entity, and your budget must give expression to your aspirations.

A budget that has estate planning in mind need not be a fearsome thing. It is an estimate of needs, a division of income, and a method of keeping control of expenditures.

Life insurance is probably the most basic tool of estate planning. There are, pared to essentials, only three basic types of life policies: term, whole life, and endowment. These are, of course, used by the estate planner in many combinations to meet his individual requirements. He shows lively interest in fitting his insurance into his present situation and needs and the future of his dependents. He does not merely buy a new policy from time to time as his income increases, but makes a program to fit his particular family needs and his resources.

Once you have decided to build an estate, using all the aids suggested here and others that you will think of, there is only one logical answer to the question, "When should I start?" The task is easier now than it will ever be again. To start is not to say, "This is it, once and forever." A proper plan is amenable to change as time brings new responsibilities and changed resources.

The act of starting provides a strong defense against worry, insecurity, financial instability, and gloom. It will not multiply your income, but it certainly will help you to stop wasteful and unrewarding leaks in your outgo. It will enable you to concentrate your firepower on the decisive targets.

You will be helped in your planning if you make a mental

picture of the way you would like your family to live, and then work toward that objective.

In doing all this planning you can be both clear-headed and gentle-hearted. In fact, it is not being gentle with one's dependents or kind to yourself to be cloudy about what life now and in the future holds in store.

We cannot evade the necessity . . . to make judgments. . . . I was discussing these matters with a young man recently and he said, "I don't mind making judgments that involve myself alone, but I object to making judgments that affect . . . other people.". I . . . had to tell him that . . . would make it impossible for him to be a second-grade teacher, a corporation president, a husband, a politician, a parent, a traffic policeman, a weatherman, a chef, a doctor or a horse-race handicapper — in fact, it would force him to live a hermit's life.

—JOHN W. GARDNER

6

The Man and His World

BETWEEN TWO WORLDS

by John B. Anderson

Representative to Congress from Illinois

The perfect society will always pass us by. Perfection in personal and social relations is something reserved for the Kingdom of God. And therefore, as Christians, we owe our ultimate responsibility toward that higher and eternal order. But our religious belief must never become a proprietary drug that we ingest so that we somehow become immune to the misery that flows all around us. This is the kind of religion which Lenin speaks of, scornfully, as the opiate of the masses. We are called to be the light of the world, the salt that gives life its savor.

Because Christians are not "of the world," they have too often tended to act as if they are not "in the world," and practiced a pietistic separation. Their separation from those things they believe to be evil has too often been an excuse for separation from those things that are good. They have often abandoned their responsibilities in the world of literature and the arts, and in the field of government itself.

One can cling to orthodox Christianity without denying the right of the poor to be clothed and fed, or the right of minorities to their civil rights, or that there is a proper role for government to assume in fighting poverty and promoting human rights. In fact, I would reverse this statement to say that it is difficult for me to believe that a Christian cannot be concerned and compassionate about these problems.

I would without hesitation maintain that man is a sinner, and that all of his social institutions are affected by sin. Ultimate social change depends upon changing men, and men cannot be changed simply by redesigning or altering the environment. If they could, Christ's death on the cross would have been completely unnecessary and the whole rationale of God's plan for man's redemption would collapse. Believing as I do that Christ's words to Nicodemus are relevant to the situation of modern man and that we must be "born again" in no way relieves me of my responsibility to pursue social justice, to act in compassion toward my fellowman, and to seek a better world. For, while man is a sinner, God has implanted within each of us a conscience, and with it we become responsible for our own actions and chargeable with the responsibility to do mercy, seek justice, and walk humbly before our God. We cannot escape the fact that we are our brother's keeper.

Thus, I think the evangelical community can be fairly criticized for its failure to devise a genuinely positive and constructive social ethic. We have been reacting against the social gospel. As an excuse for a noncontributing role, we cling to an exceedingly individualistic heritage. We suffer from "withdrawal symptoms." We have an essentially negative approach to the very real problems of many of our neighbors.

However, we can be thankful that there is an evident change of opinion and approach making itself felt within the evangelical community. Some new directions are taking shape as we rethink our obligations in and to society. To this new thrust I would like to add some thoughts on the creation of a new and vital, evangelical social ethic.

1. *We need to develop a Christian social ethic that looks both to the need of the human heart and the inner man, and to man's external relations* — to both the spiritual and the physical elements in life. We should lead the way in creating an integrated ethical system that reunites personal re-

sponsibility with social responsibility, and yet remains true to the demands of the gospel.

2. *We need a more positive outlook toward government.* As evangelicals, we have tended to have a negative attitude toward government. This, it seems to me, is contrary to Scripture, which tells us that government is an institution ordered by God as an instrument of justice. The fact that we do not regard government as the panacea for all our social ills does not mean that we fail to recognize that government is one of the fundamental orders of creation and therefore deserves our respect as Christians every bit as much as marriage and the family.

3. *We need a more realistic view of politics.* There is in American culture a sort of mythological caricature of the corrupt, calculating politician. We must recognize that politics is no more corrupt or corrupting than many other professions — that the corruption manifests itself in a different manner. In fact, it is perfectly logical to argue that politics may be less corrupt, because it is subject to public scrutiny.

There is a famous statue of the great humorist Will Rogers at the entrance to Statuary Hall in the United States Capitol. He is facing down the corridor in the direction of the House Chamber. Legend has it that he wanted to be placed in that position so that he could keep an eye on the Congress which he so often lampooned.

I wonder how many Christians reading these pages have ever held political office, even as a precinct committeeman. If Christians leave opportunities for participation open and unfilled, the void will be filled by those who do not necessarily share a similar ethical concern. We must be careful not to lose by default what could be won with some additional effort on our part.

Someone has said, "The church is filled with willing people — some of them willing to work and others willing to let them." Let none of us take refuge in the false notion that the problems of poverty and social injustice are the exclusive concern of the state.

The average American today suffers no twinge of conscience when he passes the sick man on the road. He knows he has paid the "Good Samaritan" to come along after him and take care of this rather unpleasant social obligation. But the import of Christ's teaching is very plain. He expects us to take the role of the Good Samaritan, and not delegate our Christian love and compassion and concern in every instance to a paid professional or functionary. We are enjoined to love our neighbor — not just to pay taxes to employ someone else to love our neighbor.

As a boy I sat through many an altar call for those willing to dedicate their lives to Christ on the foreign mission field. I trust that many will continue to heed a similar call, for the needs of the developing countries of the world are still great. However, I would also like to see some altar calls for men and women who would publicly dedicate themselves to help meet the needs in their home community. I believe the church needs to get very specific about this and sharpen the challenge to all of us who call ourselves Christians to really find a place of service. It may not be full time; perhaps part time in a school, hospital, or out-patient clinic. The needs are legion; they could be inventoried very quickly through the help of a local community welfare council or a Red Feather agency.

I believe a large part of the problem is the inability of the average member of an affluent suburban church to feel much real empathy for the problems of an inner-city world so remote from his own existence. I am afraid that there are a great many modern Christians who, if our Lord suddenly returned and they found him dining with the publicans and sinners who infest the big city slums, would recoil with the same fastidious horror displayed by the Pharisees and Sadducees two thousand years ago. Yet Henry Drummond, in his great sermon "The City Without a Church," reminds us:

> City life is human life at its intensest, man in his most real relations. And the nearer one draws to reality, the nearer one draws to the working sphere of religion. Wherever real life is, there Christ goes. And he goes there, not only because the great

need lies there, but because there is found, so to speak, the raw material with which Christianity works . . . the life of man. To do something with this, to infuse something into this, to save and inspire and sanctify this — the actual working life of the world — is what he came for. Without human life to act upon, without relations of men with one another, of master with servant, husband with wife, buyer with seller, creditor with debtor, there is no such thing as Christianity. With actual things, with humanity in its everyday dress, with the traffic of the streets, with gates and houses, with work and wages, with sin and poverty, with these things and all the things and all the relations and all the people of the city Christianity has to do, and has more to do than with anything else.

The Church of Jesus Christ ought to play a part in rallying Christians to social action. Indeed, it is only as we play this kind of role that we will get the type of society that we as Christians would like to see. The Church can and should encourage social and economic change. We are living in an age when, to paraphrase the late President Kennedy, every Christian should in effect be an officeholder.

I once heard President Nixon state the goals of his administration in terms of three R's. He listed them as Reorganization, Renewal, and Restoration. I'm still old-fashioned enough in my theology to believe that the three R's of the church are Redemption, Regeneration, and Renewal. We must begin to construct a new, vital, Christian social ethic and tradition which can give us the moral foundation on which to build an America capable of achieving its national goals.

Remember not only to say the right thing in the right place, but, far more difficult still, to leave unsaid the wrong thing at the tempting moment.

—BENJAMIN FRANKLIN

ISOLATION IS INSANITY

By Creath Davis

Founding Director of Christian Concern Foundation

Life was never meant to be a solitary existence. To be totally cut off emotionally from personal relationships would produce insanity.

If you have ever moved from your hometown, you have felt the pangs of being separated from those you know and love and of being thrust among strangers. Your relationships with people do more toward making you feel comfortable than your physical surroundings. You never feel at home until you are at home with someone.

Man was made for meaningful relationships. In the Genesis account, man was made in the image of God to have dominion over the rest of creation and to share in an uninhibited relationship with God. It was in the cool of the day, when evidently God was accustomed to dialoguing with Adam, that Adam hid from God because he had disobeyed. Sin had broken his uninhibited filiation with God. The rest of the Bible is the record of God's initiative in seeking to redeem this fallen creature and to reestablish a loving, trusting relationship.

Not only was man to have a meaningful relationship with his Creator who was above him, but also with his peers beside him. The first bond of union was marriage.

> And the Lord God said, It is not good that man should be alone: I will make him an help meet for him. . . . And the Lord God caused a deep sleep to fall upon Adam, and he slept; and he took one of his ribs, and closed up the flesh instead thereof; and the rib, which the Lord God had taken from man, made he a woman, and brought her unto the man. And Adam said, This is now bone of my bones, and flesh of my flesh: she shall be called Woman, because she was taken out of man. Therefore shall a man leave his father and his mother, and shall cleave unto his wife: and they shall be one flesh.

Marriage becomes the training ground for relating to another in love and openness, and furnishes the opportunity for achieving unity.

Relationships are so important that Martin Buber, in his book *I and Thou,* says that "all real living is meeting" — God and others! "The lesson of human development is that from birth to death man is always becoming a complexity of relationships. The self is a more or less fluid patterning of relationships whose change or permanence depends on the stability of the relationship of which the person is a part." The measure of life is the quality of our personal relationships. A man is only as rich or as poor personally as his relationships.

A person who in a loving, trusting relationship knows and is known by one other human being is rich indeed, and he need not fear being open to the world. Sidney Jourard says, "Every maladjusted person is a person who has not made himself known to another human being and in consequence does not know himself. Nor can he be himself. More than that, he struggles actively to avoid becoming known by another human being. He works at it ceaselessly, twenty-four hours daily; and it is work!"

Buber had delineated two kinds of relationships — the "I-Thou" and the "I-It." The I-Thou relationship is the most basic. Out of it persons emerge as persons. In the I-Thou relationship both the I and the Thou are affected. Each has a sense of his own worth as a person and values the other as well. This relationship is based upon the ability of one person to enter and share deeply the life of another, without losing his own identity or individuality. Not only does he share in the rich variety of another's personality, but in the relationship he exercises the aptitudes which make him more strikingly unique. The hidden, unexpressed qualities within each are released, and the relationship becomes richer and even more creative.

Dr. Paul Tournier illustrates the power of the person-to-person relationship. His parents died when he was young and he went to live with an aunt and uncle. His aunt was mentally ill. Dr. Tournier related how, as a result, he grew up not knowing how to relate to people. He was locked inside himself. In school a Greek professor took an interest in him and often invited young Paul home with him to sit in front of the fireplace and visit. Paul's relationship with the professor broke the bonds of his repressed inner self. He was released from being a retiring, restricted lad and became a brilliant student and a leader of a national youth movement in Switzerland.

The power of the I-Thou relationship is fantastic. Dr. Tournier was awakened to genuine personhood by it. But in an I-Thou relationship the results are never one-way — both persons are affected. Dr. Tournier said that when he wrote the manuscript for his first book, the one evaluation of it he wanted most was that of his Greek professor. So he made an appointment with the professor and went to his home. He read his first chapter with a great deal of anxiety as the old professor listened. After he finished, there was complete silence. Dr. Tournier awaited his opinion. After a few moments the professor said, "Paul, read on." He read another chapter. Again, silence. This procedure continued through the reading of the entire manuscript. After the last chapter, Dr. Tournier said the old professor looked at him and said, "Paul, I feel that we need to pray together."

"But, sir," Dr. Tournier queried, "I didn't know you were a Christian."

The professor replied calmly, "I am."

"But, since when?"

"As of this moment."

I was deeply moved as I heard Dr. Tournier relate this experience. The power of personal involvement! It struck me how much we need to present our witness in the context of meaningful, authentic relationships so we do not become peddlers of the gospel.

The other relationship that Buber mentions is the I-It relationship: "Without *It* man cannot live. But he who lives with It alone is not man." There is legitimate concern with things, using them as an expression of one's own life and creativity. The tragedy comes when we seek to relate to another person as an *It* instead of a *Thou*. To use another person as a prop for our own ego, or to manipulate him for our purposes is to relate to him as a thing and not as a person. This becomes a form of murder and suicide. In relating to human beings as things, we destroy them and ourselves as well.

The manner in which a person relates to God, to others, and to himself is a simple but accurate barometer of his life. I can understand myself best in terms of my relationships with others.

In this day when people are being crowded closer together physically but seem to be pushed further apart emotionally, the "people of God" desperately need to recapture the spirit of *koinonia,* which the New Testament believers had. *Koinonia* is the Greek word which is usually translated in English as "fellowship." This is really an extension of the I-Thou relationship, immersed in deep concern, to a larger community of people.

This community of believers has much in common. They share their common humanity; but more, they share their acknowledgment of personal rebellion against God and their reconciliation to God through Christ. They have, in fact, become the "body of Christ" in the world. God purposes through this people who have received Christ as Savior and Lord to love his world something like the way he loved it in Christ.

The Christian life was never meant to be a "lone ranger" experience. To say we do not need anyone to help us in our Christian venture is to say we do not need God to help us. Part of his way of helping us is through fellowship with his people. To abnegate fellowship is to be impoverished.

I learned the power of *koinonia* in a fellowship group in my pastorate. One middle-aged man — a railroad brakeman with a fourth-grade education — was released from his timidity and inferiority complex by the power of that fellowship. His parents had died when he was a child and he had experienced an extremely difficult childhood. As a result, he was so timid that when he went into an employment office once to apply for a job he hadn't the courage to tell the secretary his name, and he had to walk out of the office — a dejected failure. That same man, in the openness and warmth of Christian fellowship, discovered who he was and who God was. And he found that he had something unique to give to others.

The transformation was so remarkable that one of our deacons said to me, "I've been a deacon forty-seven years, but I've never seen anyone change like that man." He had such a winsome effect on his co-workers that they kept him awake at night asking questions about what had happened to him. He didn't know any better than simply to share what he was experiencing. Later he was invited to a nearby college to speak to a group of ministerial students. He was so free and open with the students that everyone had tears streaming down their cheeks when he finished. There was not one trace of timidity remaining in him! Love had cast out all fear. He had become the best communicator in our congregation — a real witness for Christ.

What those men in that fellowship group did for me cannot be overestimated. They helped me to lay aside my preacher-mask and accept myself as a fellow-struggler. We met early on Sunday mornings for a time of personal sharing and prayer. I was often so touched by the power of God to change lives, families, and vocations in that group that at times it was almost more than I could contain. I spent many of the Sunday school hours at home, literally weeping, because I was so full after our sharing time. On a couple of occasions I was so full of gratitude for what God was doing that instead of preaching I could only weep. Somehow the Lord got through those tears, and our entire congregation responded with a warmth and openness that we had never before experienced.

God help us to recover the power of fellowship!

The following is a list of some essential elements for meaningful personal relationships.

1. Meaningful relationships require two persons who are

mature enough to relate to each other on the basis of each being a person of worth and dignity.

2. Each person must have enough independence that he does not become unduly anxious when he has to stand alone.

3. Each person must have sufficient self-acceptance so that he is not driven compulsively to try to use the other person as a prop for his own ego or as a necessary tool for his own welfare.

4. Each is given the freedom to express his own uniqueness.

5. Each appreciates the other, and feels that he has something of value to give to him. There is present the ability to give and receive freely, without the sense of debt-repayment.

6. Because each is accepted as a person, there is a sense of security that stems from the fact that his acceptance is not conditional or temporary.

7. Each is aware of his own uniqueness, which is worthy of expression, and he does not seek to deny this by trying to change himself to gain the approval of others.

8. The relationship itself becomes more important than the immediate pain or pleasure of the persons involved, and can be maintained even at the cost of temporary discomforts.

9. The intrinsic quality of this kind of relationship is nothing less than love.

The surest way to keep from being related meaningfully with other people is to go out aggressively looking for "a relationship." Relax, and begin opening yourself slowly to those around you, focusing your attention upon them and their needs. If we want a friend, we must offer ourselves as a friend. If we want to be accepted and respected, then we must give acceptance and respect. If we want love, we must give love!

GOD'S MAN ON THE SPOT

by J. Allan Petersen

God needs men, young men, old men, men in their prime of life. He has chosen to do his work through men — whether scholars or laborers, kings or commoners. And God has always had his man, in every age and for every crisis — men like Daniel.

Any man whom God calls "greatly beloved" deserves our attention. And certainly any man whom God calls greatly beloved three times in the space of a few sentences deserves our special and careful attention. He can be no ordinary man to whom God would send the angel Gabriel to convey such a message of divine affection.

Why was Daniel thus favored? What made him the unusual success, the wise counselor, the dynamic leader that he was? The fascinating story is in the first chapter of the book of Daniel, and we note immediately certain characteristics that inevitably mark one of God's men. And since Daniel was about seventeen years old at this time, his life is a perennial encouragement to every young man.

First of all, *Daniel's life was marked by confidence, not conflict.* Daniel was raised in Jerusalem, the religious center of his day. He grew up in the environment of a strongly religious home. His godly parents had taught him well, and by the age of seventeen he had become a stalwart youth whose life was already committed to God.

Into the midst of this tranquil, happy scene came Nebuchadnezzar of Babylon and his invading forces. Jerusalem is besieged, the king of Judah is captured, and the choicest young men of the nation are taken captive. What a sad and violent upheaval! Family circles are shattered, the most promising children snatched away into a heathen land to face servitude, an alien culture, a totally different set of values, and a polytheistic religion. All this alone, without the support and encouragement of family and friends.

This kind of crisis will result in one of two reactions, depending on the man. It will either inspire dependence on and confidence in God, or breed inner conflict and frustration.

In reading the story, you never get the feeling that Daniel was frustrated, confused, wondering if God had made a mistake. You don't find him complaining, retreating into his shell, developing a negative attitude or persecution complex. Instead, you sense a quiet, all-pervading confidence that he was in Babylon, in the king's palace, in a heathen culture, and away from his godly family not by an unfortunate accident but by divine appointment. "God has allowed me to be in this situation. He must have a purpose. I will discover his plan and seek to live wisely here where he has placed me. God would never put me where I cannot serve him in some way. I will trust him and serve him in Babylon as well as in Jerusalem." This is quiet confidence, not questioning conflict.

A college boy came to me one night during some meetings in Canada. He said, "I've got a real problem. It's where I work. There's not another Christian in the place. I'm surrounded with tough, hard drinking, foul-mouthed men. It's swearing and dirty jokes all day long. I can't stand it! Would you pray that I can get a job where there will be only Christians and I won't have to put up with this any more?"

Without hesitation and as strongly as possible, I said, "No! I can't pray such a prayer! God needs you right there where you are! He put you there! Don't panic and run away from the tremendous opportunity that God has placed in your hands. Grasp it thankfully. Find out how to reach them. You may be the only representative Christ has to some of those men. Don't muff the ball!"

What man doesn't know from experience the nature of our world! Paul says in 2 Timothy 3:1-4: "They will love only themselves and money . . . sneering at God . . . immoral . . . cruel." In other words, this is a degraded world. Jesus reminds us in Matthew 10:16, 17 that we are in a dangerous world, and in John 17:14, 15 an evil world. Philippians 2: 14, 15 speaks of a dark, crooked, and stubborn world. This is man's world. It is here — right here in this degraded world — that we are to stand; it is here in this dangerous world that we are to serve; it is here in this dark world that we are to shine. God put us here.

Daniel's life was also marked by identification, not isolation. In the godless world situation which Daniel faced and which we also face today, there are basically two courses of action. We must either identify or isolate.

But, with what can we identify in this kind of world? With all that is morally acceptable and socially good. Only by this identifying of ourselves are we in a position to influence those around us and be of service to them. If we isolate ourselves in Christian "stockades," retreating from the harsh realities of twentieth-century living, assuming a superior and censorious view of those around us, we will remain forever spiritually sterile and useless.

Daniel elected to identify. He had been chosen for his physical and mental prowess, and he set out to develop these to the greatest advantage. He kept his body in good shape, though it required tact and persistence to accomplish it. He studied the Babylonian philosophy, their science, their politics; he became thoroughly familiar with their language and customs, gracefully accepting and using the new name they gave him, since his Jewish name was foreign and strange to them. Through all this he advanced, step by step, finally reaching the highest position in the empire under the king.

Is there anything wrong with this much identification? Obviously not in the eyes of God. Paul had exactly the same attitude as Daniel: "I have freely and happily become a servant of any and all, so that I can win them to Christ . . . when with the heathen I agree with them as much as I can, except, of course, that I must always do what is right as a Christian. And so, by agreeing, I can win their confidence and help them too" (1 Corinthians 9:17, 21, TLB).

Daniel was also a man of conviction, not compromise. It is easy to assume that the person who identifies with unbelievers has no real convictions and is compromising his

Christian testimony. This is the accusation the Pharisees hurled at Jesus. "Why," they asked his disciples, "does your Master associate with sinful men?" To which the Lord replied, "Because they who are sick need a doctor, not those who are well!" A physician must identify with his patients though he does not compromise with their diseases.

A personal opinion is one thing; a deep conviction is something else. You control your opinions, modifying, silencing, or surrendering them, depending on circumstances and your own personal comfort. A conviction, on the other hand, controls *you* and shapes your character and destiny. You will not surrender a true conviction, whatever the opposition, whatever the outcome. Men are not burned at the stake for opinions; men become martyrs because of convictions.

No sooner had Daniel arrived in the Babylonian court than he was faced with the first trial of his convictions. Food and wine were brought to the young Jewish captives — the best from the king's kitchen. But the food, Daniel knew, had been offered to idols. The wine had been poured as a libation to their heathen deities. This cut directly across his convictions. He must not partake of it, yet how could he refuse and still survive?

The eighth verse of this first chapter gives us a clue to Daniel's whole life and attitude. "Daniel purposed in his heart that he would not defile himself." This is a strong phrase: "He *purposed* in his heart." He made up his mind! Regardless of the consequences, character demands a strong purpose. God demands decisive men. Some of my personal preferences and practices may not be very important, but my principles regarding personal honesty, integrity, morality, purity — these are not up for change or compromise.

Daniel was also marked by amiableness, not antagonism. In his handling of the very delicate problem of the king's food and wine, Daniel showed not only unflinching conviction, but kindness and courtesy, not only honorableness but humility. He did not flaunt his religious beliefs, demanding that a heathen respect them; rather he requested that he and his Jewish companions be served a different diet on a trial basis. He made his request clearly and thoughtfully, outlining a specific, workable plan. And he did it confidently, assured that the God who had brought him into this situation would not let him down. His commitment would not allow him to be cantankerous.

Jesus said, "Blessed are they which are persecuted for *righteousness'* sake," not for negative decisions. So often we compound our difficulties by an exacting and judgmental attitude which reveals our own *self*-righteousness. Doors that God has opened are closed by our tactlessness and pride. When the right stand is taken in the wrong way, our entire witness is canceled and our good is evil spoken of. Christ was never criticized for his manner but only for his message. Daniel, too, had such an excellent spirit, free from fear and characterized by power, love, and self-control.

Finally, *Daniel's life was marked by exaltation, not extinction.* His unswerving loyalty to God did not relegate him to oblivion. Rather, because he handled his problems with wisdom and graciousness he opened the hearts of his captors, commanding their respect and admiration.

The story of another man in Genesis 39 also shows how testing was the preparation for exaltation. Joseph was misunderstood, maligned, unjustly imprisoned, and to outward appearances forgotten even by God. But he waited, uncomplaining, for divine wisdom to stem the tide of injustice and bring to fulfillment the dreams of greatness with which God had stirred his eager heart in boyhood days. The psalmist tells us: "There in prison they hurt his feet with fetters and placed his neck in an iron collar." But as Joseph patiently wore the iron on his neck, God was imparting iron into his soul. And the lesson is clear that his rise to royalty was not in spite of but because of the sufferings he endured and the trials he met and conquered.

God's time came. In one day, in one swift dramatic moment, Joseph was whisked out of the dungeon to the throne room, out of disgrace into honor, out of servitude into service to God and man. God had not forgotten — he never forgets. He waits and he works on all the circumstances, preparing us for what he has prepared for us.

Daniel too, met this test — and many tests. In fact, his life could well fit the statement concerning a young lad made five hundred years later: "Jesus increased in wisdom and stature, and in favor with God and man." By divinely inspired wisdom and diplomacy, Daniel rose step by step to the position of Prime Minister, a place he held until he was ninety years old. He started well and ended strongly as a classic example of God's eternal principle: "Them that honor me I will honor" (1 Samuel 2:30).

What happened to Daniel was not as important as what he did with what happened. Perplexing problems he handled with poise; bitter opposition he conquered with courage and decision; malicious threat and physical danger he faced with faith and fortitude. What a man! He was God's man in the world!

COMMUNICATING

What I can do to share my faith and support my church:

Have phone	*will call.*
Have pen	*will write.*
Have interest	*will come.*
Have car	*will bring.*
Have money	*will tithe.*
Have voice	*will witness.*
Have concern	*will pray.*
Have love	*will share.*

GROWING WITH PEOPLE

by R. Lofton Hudson

Director, Midwest Christian Counseling Center, Kansas City, Missouri

Every man is a problem in search of a solution. We are born into a world that is autocratic, that is, from the very first we are pushed around, given orders, bossed, made to conform. And the child's problem is to learn how to move from an autocratic world to a democratic one. We must learn how to boss ourselves instead of being bossed — and it is a slow, painful process.

Children grow only as they learn how to solve problems which are gradually pitched into their laps. Learning to get along with people is one problem with which every one of us must deal. It is certainly necessary to happiness, usefulness, and success. It is even necessary to survival.

"Learn" is the key word. Jesus said, "Unless you turn and become like children, you will never enter the kingdom of heaven." Children grow in their ability to get along with people. Unless we adults retrace our steps and unlearn some of our bad personal habits, open our minds to new patterns of conduct, there is no hope for us. Growth is not only "adding to" but also relearning. I have seen people sixty years of age "turn" and learn how to follow Jesus in dealing with people.

One of the ways of improving our relations with our fellows is to look at some of the faulty techniques we use. The interesting thing about them, too, is that they all are dealt with in the New Testament. There never has been such a valuable book on human relations.

Scapegoating. A scapegoat is anybody we blame for the trouble we are in. Hitler blamed the Jews for all of the deprivations he forced upon the people as he built up a war economy. As the Roman Empire crumbled, the Christians were blamed. In the Old Testament, Ahab said to Elijah,

"Art thou he that troubleth Israel?" It is hard for those who are failing to honestly analyze the reasons for failure and to change what is wrong. It is so much easier to blame someone else.

The halo technique. Closely associated with scapegoating is the "halo" technique. This is the practice of being perfect. One of my friends illustrated this humorously in the words, "I am not the least bit conceited, but I don't know why I am not." Jesus pointed out this type in the person who says, "Let me help you get that speck out of your eye," while all the time there was a whole beam in the speaker's eye. He dramatized the technique by telling of a man who stood and prayed, "God, I thank thee, that I am not as other men are . . . even as this publican." Pardon me while I adjust my halo! "Confess your faults one to another and pray for one another" (James 5:16).

Labeling. Another method which often destroys good human relations is the "labeling" technique. All of us hate to be called names. And some people never seem to realize that they can get just as bad results as a "cusser" without being profane. A man may not slap you for calling him narrow-minded, prudish, naive, or an old fogy, but he won't like you. The trouble with labels, you see, is that they are used to describe individuals as if that were all there is to the person. For example, "Smith is a neurotic." Is he neurotic all the time? And just wherein is he different from you or me? Smith may be honest, industrious, religious, and unselfish too.

Labels are devices used by talkative people to save them the trouble of thinking. Jesus warned against this hateful manner of speaking: "Whosoever shall say to his brother, . . . thou fool, shall be in danger of hell fire" (Matthew 5:22).

In the doghouse. One of the most common ways of losing friends and hurting people is the "doghouse" technique. You make a mistake or give offense and you are ostracized for life.

Some people relegate whole classes of society to the dog-house. They differ economically, sometimes racially, sometimes socially, sometimes religiously. These superior beings will not associate with the "low brows" even if they try to grow. It is a modern form of the ancient heresy: "The Jews have no dealings with the Samaritans."

I'll-take-my-dolls-and-go-home. This is another antisocial technique which all of us have practiced at one time or other. Our feelings are hurt, and we resign, or get a divorce, or quit a job.

Even in church this conduct is sometimes seen. I have known people to drift from one church to another because they got their feelings hurt in each new group and nursed deep injuries. It is easier to move on than it is to grow up.

Divorces are oftener than not the result of this "I'll-take-my-dolls-and-go-home" reaction. A large percent of couples who separate could learn to live together if they did not resort to this revenge method. It is the easy — though childish — way. And as long as society adds its blessings to the "incompatibility" and "mental cruelty" types of divorce, people will be encouraged to remain immature.

Principles of Good Human Relations

Communication. When relations get bad between nations they "break off communication" and recall their ambassadors. It is just as true within family circles. I have known husbands and wives who would not speak to each other. At the breakfast table the father would say, "Jimmie, tell your mother to pass me the bacon." Sometimes we become so mad that we do not trust ourselves to talk. A man will say, "I would have gone to see the man and tried to talk it out with him, but I was afraid I would say something I would regret."

About the meanest sort of refusal to communicate is to refrain from the common courtesy of speaking to people. One of the shrewdest statements the late George Bernard Shaw ever wrote was: "The worst sin towards our fellow creatures is not to hate them but to be indifferent to them. That's the essence of inhumanity."

Jesus placed communication as the basic means of good relations. "If thou bring thy gift to the altar, and there rememberest that thy brother hath aught against thee; leave there thy gift before the altar, and go thy way; first be reconciled to thy brother, and then come and offer thy gift" (Matthew 5:23, 24). "If thy brother shall trespass against thee, go and tell him his fault between thee and him alone; if he shall hear thee, thou hast gained thy brother" (Matthew 18:15). The common factor in settling differences, whether one has offended or has been offended, is to talk it out. The Christian is to renew communications, whether the difficulty is in the church or between labor and capital, husband and wife, father and son, or business associates. I have known PhD.'s on university campuses who would not speak to each other. So regardless of education or social class, the principle is the same: communication is a prime essential in good human relations.

Group authority. A second principle of good relations is to let the group decide.

This is precisely what Jesus said. In the passage in Matthew 18, we are directed to talk first to the offender alone; if fruitless, we are to take one or two witnesses; the third step is to "tell it to the church." The two last steps involve the very understandable fact that individuals need the counsel of the group. A consensus of opinion as authority is inherent in democracy.

Of course, the majority opinion will not always represent the truth — perhaps seldom, in some fields — but it must be recognized if people are to get along together.

"I want your advice" or "I'd like to discuss a matter with you" are words of humility. We need to check our opinions on morals, religion, politics, and any other subject by discussing them with our fellows. As we come alive in Christ, we will know that only the group which has a similar experience will be able to counsel us on matters pertaining to the kingdom of God. In some situations only God can guide us in the true way. "Let God be true, but every man a liar" (Romans 3:4) was the Apostle Paul's priority.

Tolerance. A third principle of good human relations is tolerance — the opposite of domination and criticism. It applies to normal relations between adults. The tolerant attitude says: "I accept you as the unique person you are. You may chart your own course, make your own mistakes, say what you really feel, and you will not be frowned at or criticized unless you attempt to hurt or destroy someone."

Nothing but faith in individuals and in God can undergird this attitude.

Jesus gives us many examples in the way he dealt with people. Peter was warned but not browbeaten concerning his denial. The Pharisees were exposed and told of their destiny because they were destroying life. But Jesus dined in the home of Simon the Pharisee and welcomed an interview with Nicodemus. And did any leader ever show as much patience and acceptance as he did toward Peter and other erring disciples? Jesus' method was exactly the opposite of the "doghouse" technique.

Forgiveness. The last principle in getting along with people handles situations where injuries, real or seeming, have occurred. And occur they will. The finest people in this world are sensitive people who are hurt deeply when they are misunderstood, who really want to love and to be loved.

We remember that Jesus said that we must be willing to forgive an unlimited number of times (Matthew 18:21, 22). Furthermore, he said that we can be forgiven our sins only as we forgive others (Matthew 6:14, 15). Thus some people have been wasting time praying for forgiveness of their sins. They may have withheld punishment from those who have hurt them, but that is not forgiveness.

Forgiveness involves three things. First, the person who has been injured accepts the injury. In order to do this, he must be mature enough to be honest about his injury and mature enough to accept suffering. Second, forgiveness may mean helping the offender bear the burden of his sin. Joseph said to his brothers who had sold him into slavery, "Be not grieved or angry with yourselves." Third, forgiveness restores the broken fellowship and understanding.

These examples are illustrated in the cross. In accepting forgiveness through the cross, we come to see that God accepts the injury of our sin, relieves us of our guilt, and brings us into a close relationship with himself.

Those who never seek or offer forgiveness relate to others on a very superficial basis or they disobey God in not rebuilding disturbed relationships. Some husbands and wives drift apart and never get close again because they do not forgive. We are such sinners that we must again and again ask one another to forgive. Only in this way can the power of God be fully experienced in human life.

Every person should have three conversions. A man needs to be converted to Jesus Christ: "Believe on the Lord Jesus Christ, and thou shalt be saved, and thy house" (Acts 16:31); to the church: "Not forsaking the assembling of ourselves together" (Hebrews 10:25); and finally converted back to the world: "Go ye into all the world, and preach the gospel to every creature" (Mark 16:15).

—GEORGE INGLE

HOW TO FAIL SPECTACULARLY

by Kermit Lueck

Business and Institutional Consultant

We hear a great deal today about the laws of success, and self-help books are a booming business, but how about our right to fail? Is there a scientific method to insure failure? We know that the only way to become successful is on purpose, but is it possible to be a failure on purpose? An exhaustive survey taken recently disclosed the fact that only three percent of all Americans are "outstandingly successful," that sixty-eight percent are "moderately successful" and twenty-nine percent of our people are "complete failures," achieving nothing.

Two tramps were sitting on a park bench discussing the economic situation, and one said to the other, "This depression don't bother me none . . . I was a failure during the boom." How can we guarantee our failure even during times of unprecedented prosperity?

A few years ago I was privileged to interview a man who spent his life researching the lives of successful men and women. The late Napoleon Hill, who had over 1,000 pupils on the millionaire and multimillionaire level, told me that he had never met a man or woman in his entire life who had risen above mediocrity without having a goal in life. So rule one for failure is:

Be a drifter — avoid like poison any short-range, intermediate, or long-range goal.

The *Wall Street Journal*, faced with the complaint that high taxes make it impossible for anyone to rise from rags to riches as the Horatio Alger heroes did, made a study that disclosed there have been more new millionaires starting from nothing in the past decade than in any other period in history. In reviewing the history of these people, I was struck by the fact that they were all different in many ways except that they were decisive. So rule number two for failure is:

Procrastinate — they even have a slogan for Procrastination Week: This Is National Procrastination Week — Don't Put It Off, Procrastinate Today!

Another good method is never to do today what you can put off until tomorrow. If you get a sudden urge to "do it now" just sit down until the mood leaves you.

Research conducted by Columbia University disclosed the amazing fact that it is not aptitudes but attitudes that make us successful. Ninety-three percent of our success is attitudes and seven percent is skill and knowledge. So failure rule number three is:

Be negative — you can catch more flies with honey than with vinegar, but who needs them?

Dr. Norman Vincent Peale told me that if you want to be successful, think success. So if you want to be a failure, think failure.

Bob Richards, the Olympic pole vaulting champion and one of our nation's great motivators, told me he believes the biggest problem facing us today is communication. That reminds me of the story of two brothers who vied with each other at Christmas time to see who could give their mother the most unusual present. One year Bill learned that Tom was giving a custom-built Cadillac. As Bill was passing a pet store he saw a parrot with a price tag of $10,000 on the cage. He asked the manager why there was such a fantastic price on the bird. He was told this was a very rare parrot that could speak seventeen languages fluently. Delighted, Bill purchased the bird and shipped it to his mother, convinced he had topped his brother for sure. He could hardly wait until Christmas Day to call and see how she liked it. He said, "Mother, how did you like the bird?"

She said, "It was delicious."

"Delicious!" he screamed. "Mother, that bird was rare . . . it cost me $10,000 and it speaks seventeen languages."

"Well, why didn't it say something then?" said his mother.

So rule number four for failure is:

Be a poor communicator — be a poor listener; even a fool is considered sensible when he keeps his mouth shut, so yak up a storm and remove all doubt.

Dr. Maxwell Maltz, the famous plastic surgeon and author of *Psycho-Cybernetics,* discovered that all of our actions are consistent with our inner opinions about ourselves. The picture that we have inside about ourselves, whether it is true or false, determines what we can or cannot do in life. So rule number five for failure is:

Sell yourself short — remind yourself constantly about all of your weaknesses, shortcomings, and past failures . . . and don't forget to tell others. Be a blob.

Jay Beecroft, world training director of Minnesota Mining and Manufacturing Company, discovered that the biggest problem facing management was motivation. Jay said people did things for "their" reasons and not "our" reasons. Ten basic drives make people tick; if we discover the strong ones, we can motivate ourselves to action. So failure rule number six is:

Fizzlemanship — when you get that "hot button" urge to achieve, fizzle! We had the pleasure of visiting with the "Sizzle Himself," Elmer Wheeler. He has motivated people with his famous slogan, "Don't sell the steak . . . sell the sizzle." If failure is your goal, however, don't sizzle . . . fizzle.

The late Ben Sweetland said that worry prevents our doing the very thing that would remove the worry. So failure rule number seven is:

Be a worry wart — a neurotic is a person who worries about things in the past that never happened, unlike the normal person who worries about things in the future that never happen! If you run out of things to fear, you can fear fear itself!

How do we fail in life without trying? The answer is in failure rule number eight:

Don't try — if at first you don't succeed, forget it! You can't win with this one. Earl Nightingale said that everyone is a self-made man, but only the successful ones admit it. Failures of the World, Unite! You Have Nothing to Lose but Your Life!

TIE THAT LOOSENS

You can't have genuine, Spirit-filled living without the loosening of purse strings. When the Lord opens our heart, then we should open our purse. Generosity to the Lord's work is economic evidence that we have been redeemed. It has been said, "You can give without loving, but you can't love with giving."

—LESLIE B. FLYNN

RESPONDING TO CHALLENGE

by Bob Richards

Former Olympic Champion

We live in the most challenging hour of all time. I think that's obvious to anyone who knows history or who knows the gigantic problems that men are grappling with today. Depending upon the responses that you and I make, so will go the next ten, twenty, thirty years, if there are those thirty years.

Arnold Toynbee, in his amazing ten-volume history of civilization, says that you can measure civilization by studying the responses of the people of history to the great challenges they have had to face; that history is only the record of how they faced one crisis after another.

As we have responded, so has history taken its course. When we have responded negatively, progress has slowed down, cultures have disintegrated, empires have collapsed. When we have responded positively, mankind has leaped ahead; art, music, religion and industry have flourished; life has been more abundant. The way we react to our challenges determines the destiny of our lives, our country, and our world.

We have nine million chronic alcoholics in America. One in three homes has a divorce. One out of thirteen of us is a mental case. Juvenile crime is increasing. Tranquilizer pills, aspirins by the tons, are being consumed. In the last ten years, the world has spent over one trillion dollars on weapons of war, and many become obsolete soon after they are made. Fear grips the world.

And how do we respond to these challenges? We can respond negatively. That is so easy! We can respond by saying, "There is really nothing that I can do; after all, I am just one little person in a vast world of social forces and struggles for power. What can I do?"

If you are prone to doubt what you can do as an individual, think of Karl Marx writing *Das Kapital* by candle-light. Think of two little disciples — unknown to the world — Lenin and Trotsky; in less than forty years these three men won half the world to Communism.

Or, on the creative side, think of men like Moses and David. Think of a man like Abraham Lincoln, of other individuals who have stood on their principles in the critical hours of history and have changed the world.

There are youngsters today who will change the world tomorrow. We must encourage them, build in them true ideas, and we must remember that ideas are no good at all except in the minds of individuals. Causes have no emotion at all except in the emotion and passion of individuals. If we will work with the minds of young boys and girls, with their emotions and values, we and they can alter human history.

Ultimately, everything depends upon the individual. Don't respond by saying there is nothing you can do. Don't respond with the hysteria of fear. Nor can we respond with the philosophy of "Eat, drink, and be merry, for tomorrow we die." That way lies disaster.

May I draw a lesson from the world of sports? I think sports come to grips with life; in some of these great stories you can see into the heart of human society. In sport, the first demand is that the athlete respond quickly. Immediately!

I think of Herb Elliott, the great miler from Australia. In Australia quite a few years ago, Elliott had a broken foot; he hadn't been running for several months. He watched John Landy run the mile under four minutes. He went up to Coach Percy Cerutty, one of the best coaches in Australia, and said, "Mr. Cerutty, I want to run the mile in less than four minutes."

Cerutty looked at him and said, "Son, do you know what it takes to run a mile under four minutes? Do you know what it is to run until you can hardly stand up, to suck in hot air until you're almost unconscious? Do you know what it is to run that kind of a race?".

Elliot said, "I don't care what it takes; I want to run the mile under four minutes."

The coach said, "OK, come out to the track tomorrow."

But Cerutty didn't put him on the track; he took him out to a beach nearby, ran him uphill on the sand, and ran him over boulders and rocks. He ran him over the most difficult obstacle course he could find. The kid kept running; he wouldn't give up.

Less than one year later, I watched nineteen or twenty-year-old Elliott run the mile in 3:54.5, to smash the world's record. That's what can happen when a man responds, when he gets a vision, when he believes that there is something that he can do.

Goethe put it so beautifully in these words: "Are you in earnest? Choose this very moment. Beginning has magic, power, boldness in it. The mind grows heated." Respond *now;* you don't know what you can do until you have made an immediate response to a challenge.

Carl Erskine is a good friend of mine. He told me once about his greatest experience in baseball. In a world series, Brooklyn was ahead two games to one and leading the third game 5 to 2. A hitter came up to the plate and Carl walked him. Another fellow came up and Carl walked him. Then big Johnnie Mize stepped up with two men on. Carl pitched one in the wrong spot and Johnnie boomed the ball into the outfield seats. The score was tied.

Carl said to me, "Bob, I can't tell you how I felt at that moment — I knew I had let my teammates down, that in that crucial moment I hadn't come up to what I should have been."

Coach Charlie Dressen came off the bench and said, "Carl, how do you feel?"

He said, "I think I am all right." Actually, he felt very low, Carl told me.

Dressen took him by the arm and said, "Carl, you're my man; I am leaving you in. You can do it!"

Carl said, "Bob, to know that he believed in me, to know that my teammates were behind me — well, I knew I *had* to come through." He retired the next sixteen men in order, and three days later the Dodgers won the series behind his brilliant pitching.

I wonder how many men have been changed by just such a touch on the shoulder? I wonder how many people have been transformed with that touch of faith? I think this may be the great need in our homes today. Instead of the tension and gnawing, we need this touch of faith. I wonder if it isn't what needs to happen between parents and children: the touch of a parent's hand saying, "I believe in you." How the world needs it!

I think of Babe Didrikson, who won two gold medals in the Olympic Games. She was All-American in softball, basketball, horseback riding, tennis, golf, swimming, and then — cancer. At the height of her career, cancer! She called in her pastor the day before she died and said, "Pray a little harder. I'm getting a little closer." The pastor prayed, and left. I played golf with her husband, and he told me the story himself of how she called him to her bedside, took him by the hand and said, "Honey, I hope you will find someone to love you as much as I have loved you." And then, as he cried like a baby, she gripped his hand as tightly as she could and said, "Now, honey, don't take on so. While I've been in the hospital, I have learned one thing. A moment of happiness is a lifetime, and I have had a lot of happiness. I have had a lot of it."

That's courage! It goes to the heart of things. To stress the quality of life rather than just quantity, to meet life's greatest tragedy with a smile, saying, "I have had a lot of great moments of happiness" — this is courage! I believe that every one of us, in some way or another, must meet life with this principle. You've got to go back into the fight and keep on going, keep on pitching, to conquer the tragedy and live a creative, useful life.

7

The Man and His God

SEARCH FOR THE ULTIMATE

by Lambert Dolphin, Jr.

Author and Lecturer

As a research physicist confronted every day with the mysteries of space and the atom, I continue to be amazed at the complexity and order of our universe. From the submicroscopic atom to the expanding galaxies, our universe runs like intricate clockwork according to physical principles which never falter.

I grew up in a small town in Idaho. Like most American kids, I was sent to Sunday school and church. But I saw the world around me as a rapidly changing, scientific marvel, and church seemed a bit out-of-date. Soon I no longer took either God or the Bible seriously.

As a lad of fourteen I decided to pursue a career in physics. Surely, science and reason would provide the ultimate answers for my life in a universe which had come into existence by chance.

But in college I had a continuing sense of emptiness. Although I studied hard and my diploma read "with high honors and distinction," I knew that I had failed to find what I was really looking for. I took up physics in graduate school, learning even more of the intricacies of the atom. I was awed once more.

The explanations of higher mathematics constantly suggested other dimensions and unseen worlds beyond sensory limits. Yet, somehow, I was not part of all this. As near as I could tell, this was a cold, impersonal universe.

After graduate school I became a research physicist, exploring the problems of space and the earth's upper atmosphere. Soon I was making more money than I had ever dreamed possible, with time for travel and friends.

Having concluded there was no God, I believed that moral standards were relative and that philosophies of life were arbitrary. I spent my spare time in search of pleasure. But as the years slipped by, I realized that my philosophy of life simply did not work.

I talked at length with a close friend of Jewish background who was going into psychiatry. He suggested that a psychiatrist might be able to help me. I had already thought of seeking such help, for alcohol had become a real problem. I was spending entire weekends "partying it up" — and nursing hangovers with fresh drinks.

I found a psychoanalyst who worked with me for nearly two and one-half years. I learned a lot about myself. Yet psychoanalysis did not change me into a different person.

I began to read psychology and found Sigmund Freud fascinating. He had constructed an elaborate theory to explain away the God of the Bible — yet he admitted he admired those rare individuals who had faith in God.

The writings of Carl Jung began to interest me next. He was much more tolerant of religion. He suggested that the individual who tried to live a strictly materialistic life soon endangered his mental health and well-being. He recognized man's religious needs and the power of the Christian faith to hold in check the forces of evil.

I began to read and study the religions of the Orient, but my search brought no satisfying answers. Finally I reached a point of despair. "No matter how many friends you have," I thought, "or how much money, or what kind of success, all will come crashing down into nothingness on the day you meet death."

From time to time in my life, I had associated with people

who were Christians, but I had always believed them to be narrow-minded and prejudiced. In spite of my resentment at their beliefs, some of them had been my best friends, I had to admit. One day some Christian friends invited me to church. Reluctant to hear another irrelevant sermon, I went along to hear the music and to please them.

I had always called myself "open-minded," but I had never actually read the Bible. I thought I knew all the answers. Now I began to read it. I saw a description of the human race which began to convince me that man is not as great as he thinks he is! It said, "All have sinned and come short of the glory of God" (Romans 3:23). That certainly was true of me, I had to admit.

One fall afternoon I called the pastor of the church I had attended. He said he could not see me that day as his dad had just died and he had to make some funeral arrangements. If my dad had just died, I'd have headed for the nearest bar and become dead drunk. The fact that this pastor was not grief-stricken made me think he must have hated his father and was glad he had died.

The next afternoon the pastor told me of the close relationship between him and his dad. He loved his father deeply. And he was confident they would be reunited in another life beyond the grave.

"This man is deluded," I thought. "Any scientist will tell you that heaven is a myth, not a reality."

The pastor asked if I were a Christian.

I told him that evidently I was not, for I didn't go to church on Sunday and morally I was sure we had quite different standards.

"Would you like to become a Christian?" he asked.

After thinking a moment I said, "No." I knew my psychiatrist would ask me to examine my motives, and I was a big enough hypocrite already. But as long as the hour was mine I began to ask some questions. One by one, he gave me the answers right out of that Book I'd never read.

My first question was, "Who is God, and how does a person get through to him?"

Quietly, he leafed through the pages of his Bible, then handed it to me and said, "Read the fifth and sixth verses of this second chapter of First Timothy."

I read: "For there is one God, and there is one mediator between God and men, the man Christ Jesus, who gave himself a ransom for all. . . ."

Again the pages flipped over and he said, "Now look here." Again I read: "Jesus said to him, 'I am the way, and the truth, and the life; no one comes to the Father, but by me' " (John 14:6).

I argued that I did not have the capacity to love God. Again, the swish of turning pages. "In this is love, not that we loved God but that he loved us . . ." (1 John 4:10).

"But I can't do what God expects of me," I argued.

This time the answer came from Ephesians 2:8, 9 — "For by grace you have been saved through faith; and this is not your own doing, it is the gift of God — not because of works, lest any man should boast."

I began to wonder if there might not be a God after all, a God big enough to understand me, able to help me with my problems.

The truth began to dawn on me. Although I called myself a scientist, I had never tried the simple experiment of praying to God and asking him to make himself real to me — if he did exist.

I quit fighting down inside and "let go." Quietly I prayed to God, asking him to enter my heart and take over my life. I asked to know his presence and help and forgiveness.

I was flooded in that instant with the love of Jesus Christ, our Lord — an overwhelming sense of God in and with me.

As I drove home, tears of joy streamed down my face. Jesus Christ was living in me! What my Christian friends had been trying to tell me was literally true. There really is a God of love who runs the universe, who is anxious to meet anyone who will invite him into his life.

My habits didn't change overnight nor did all my doubts suddenly disappear. But the Bible brought deep insights into myself which I had never found elsewhere. Jesus Christ cleansed me of my guilt and sin and brought me peace and power and joy — which years of psychoanalysis had failed to do.

That was twelve years ago. Since then, as a scientist, I have repeatedly put the Bible to the test in the laboratory of life. I am fully convinced that this remarkable document is precisely what it claims to be: the Word of God.

I have endeavored to know many things deemed worth knowing among men. But with all my acquisition of knowledge, nothing comforts me now at the close of my life except the saying of the Apostle Paul, "Christ Jesus came into the world to save sinners; of whom I am chief" (1 Timothy 1:15).

—SELDEN

SUPREME SURRENDER

by Albert Hughes

Late Author and Lecturer

Apart from the Lord Jesus Christ, the Apostle Paul is the foremost figure in the history of Christianity. Paul's personality, his preaching, his writing — all of it by the Holy Spirit — has helped to make Christianity a world power.

It is an interesting fact that the library of the Theological School in Harvard University contains more than two thousand volumes dealing with the life and letters of the Apostle Paul, which averages more than one volume each year since Paul's day. In addition to these two thousand volumes, there are thousands of histories and commentaries in which the life and teaching of Paul occupy an important place. From these facts alone it could be adjudged that here was a man who was tremendously influential and is worthy of our keenest attention. We might well ask what some of the elements were that made Paul so mighty in his own day, and even in ours.

Many Christians consider that conversion is the climax and consummation of Christianity. From the study of Paul's life, we find this is not so. If ever a soul knew God's salvation, Saul of Tarsus did through his supernatural encounter with Christ on the road to Damascus. But accompanying his salvation came this other supreme step — surrender. Saul saw what we all need to see: that Jesus Christ has gone on from the cross to the grave to the glory, and that he is the living Lord at the Father's right hand. It is here that the majority of believers are spiritually myopic. Christianity is not a dynamic force in their lives because Christ is not a constant reality to them.

"The demons also believe and tremble" at the great objective facts of God and of Christ, but only those who daily apply Christ's cleansing blood and depend upon his indwelling power rejoice in victory.

As the objective facts of the cross, the resurrection, and the ascension of Christ became experiential realities in Saul's soul, he was completely changed. Seeing these wonders and claiming them for himself, Saul surrendered totally to the one who had forgiven and cleansed his past. He committed all he had and hoped for into the hands of the One he had been persecuting, and ever afterward called him "Lord."

Saul's surrender was two-fold: "Lord, what wilt thou have me to do?" It was the surrender to a new mastery and to a new ministry. He got a new Captain and entered upon a new conquest. From henceforth he had a new Lord and a new life, a new Savior and a new service, a new Boss and a new business.

It came at high noon. Pressing toward Damascus with an impassioned haste, Saul would not permit his company to rest even during the intolerable blaze of the Syrian sun. But suddenly they were halted: a great light shining more splendidly than the sun smote them all to the ground. It was the splendor of the glory of God as seen in the face of Jesus Christ.

Out of that blaze of light came a Voice — the same Voice which of old Moses heard out of the bush that burned but was not consumed. "Saul, Saul, why persecutest thou me?"

"Who art thou, Lord?" Did Saul suppose for a single moment that the answer could be given him in a sentence? A whole lifetime would not be sufficient for such a revelation. It can come only gradually, even as the dawn breaks over the wide-spreading landscape. Even an eternity would fail to make known all that he is.

"I am Jesus" was as complete an answer as Saul could perceive that day. "We know in part" and only in part. But Saul learned that the One he had seen in that effulgent glory was the Jesus of Nazareth who had been crucified and was dead and buried. To that One Saul supremely surrendered, and immediately declared him Lord and Master. From that decision he never deviated. The fullness of that conviction became the force for all his future life.

This yielding to the new mastery does not come easily.

Only the might of God can accomplish it. Saul, the greatest living antagonist of Christ, was plunging madly, hotly, anxiously ahead on that Damascus road. He had to be halted, captured, harnessed, brought under control. He was by no means ready for it. But the inevitable surrender to the all-powerful Jesus of Nazareth took place, and Saul went on the rest of his journey calling him Lord.

This is the outstanding need in all our churches today — people who recognize the Lordship of Christ and yield to his mastery. Give us Christians like these and our church problems are immediately solved. There is only one proper place for us to put Christ if we profess to love him, and that place is *first*. All the mischief of the devil and all the bankruptcy and heartache in our own experience come because we fail at this point. May the Holy Spirit convict us of that.

We have such superficial views of spiritual progress. There are numerous congregations who imagine that they could exercise a mighty influence over their area if they only had a better or larger building. They plunge themselves into a huge debt, only to discover they have no more attraction than before, but they have a much heavier burden.

Again, churches report progress when they have added a few people. What a fallacy! Adding people may be a great calamity. Adding soldiers does not always mean victory to an army; it depends upon the type of soldier you add, the equipment you give, and the training supplied as to whether you have added strength.

God has demonstrated that he can shake the world with a yielded man: a Moses, an Elijah, a Peter, a Paul, a Luther, a Wesley, a Finney, a Moody, an Evan Roberts, and he is waiting for another man. Who is that man to be? You or I?

"Quit you like *men*" — not fops, dolls, dandies, prigs, hypocrites, or halfhearted pretenders! Give us men who know God and are known of God, and even yet a nation and an empire can be stirred from center to circumference.

A Saul of Tarsus who yields to Christ can make kings murmur, "Almost thou persuadest me to be a Christian."

Let us see that the outstanding need everywhere is for men and women, boys and girls who will make Christ Master, Controller, Dictator, King. Right at the start Saul of Tarsus saw the supreme need for that and surrendered splendidly to the Savior who had soundly saved him. Until then he had been under the mastery of his own conscience, his own hot heart, his personal hatreds and prejudices, the dictates of the religious high priest. But now the die was cast, the Rubicon was crossed, and he went over for good to the opposition and made that the governing side of his life, proclaiming Jesus Christ absolute Master. Later on we hear him say, in triumph, "To me to live is Christ." What he meant was: "I want no thoughts but his thoughts, no plan but his plan, no will but his will, no hopes but his hope, no spirit but his Spirit. It is all Christ, first, last, and all the time. My time is not mine, my energy is not mine, my eyes are not mine, my feet are not mine, my blood is not mine, my tongue is not mine, my brain is not mine, my house is not mine, my business is not mine, my money is not mine. He created me, died for me, lives for me, keeps me, comes for me. O Christ Jesus, thine, only thine would I be now and forevermore."

Make Christ Master and he will make you master. Make him King and you will be a better grocer, a better butcher, a better baker, a better candlestick maker — a better anything. In this way Christianity will become radiant and attractive. The lost will want a faith like this.

May God speed the day to us when whatever we do we do it to the glory of God. We can glorify him at the typewriter, at the beach, in the school, at home, at play, on the ladder painting the house, in the mine digging coal, or, like William Carey, cobbling shoes. This will be possible the moment we make Christ Master. Are you ready?

From *Renamed — Saul Becomes Paul*, by Albert Hughes, American Bible Conference Association, Inc., 601 Drexel Bldg., Philadelphia

THE PRICELESS HOUR

by Dr. L. Nelson Bell

Editor and Former Medical Missionary

There is only one way to a healthy Christian life. I am not talking about how we become Christians: that is through faith in Jesus Christ and in no other way. But it is a fact that the average Christian shows little to distinguish him from unbelievers about him. Like those in the Chinese proverb who are "rich men living like beggars," the average Christian is living in spiritual poverty when he should be reveling in the fullness of God's grace. With the revelation of God's wisdom at hand, he nonetheless grovels in the sophisticated ignorance of worldly sentiments.

This should not be so. By using the "means of grace" available to us, we will find that a loving heavenly Father has made complete provision for our daily living and abiding relationship in him. He offers us the peace and joy reserved for the Christian alone as well as compassion for and usefulness to those about us.

There is no substitute in the Christian life for a consistent, daily, devotional time. Without it, days can prove chaotic and nights be filled with restless foreboding.

What do I mean by daily devotions? A time when I surrender my mind, will, and body to the supernatural presence and teaching of God, my heavenly Father, to Christ, my Savior and Lord, and to the Holy Spirit, my Comforter and Guide. It is a time when I can rest in God, wait on him, listen to him, and talk with him.

Many Christians think of prayer solely in terms of asking God for things or for emergency help. Actually, prayer is a two-way communication between God and us. Our prayer should not be an arrangement of stilted phrases, but natural conversation as one would talk to a loved one. It should include worship, praise, petition, and thanksgiving. There may be a statement of a problem, as when King Hezekiah took the threatening letter of the Assyrians and "spread it before the Lord . . . and prayed" (2 Kings 19:8-19). And there is the claiming of God's promises with reference to any problems we are having.

Our petitions include those personal matters that seem so large to us and yet are very simple for God. They include requests for others and their problems. And they include broader concerns about such matters as those who make and administer laws, the witness of the gospel in every land, and the moral conditions through which Satan would make a hell on this earth.

What about the daily reading of the Bible? Like the charts of the pilot, the maps of the traveler, so is the Bible to the Christian. In this Spirit-given Book we learn of the nature of God, his perspective on time and eternity, and his will for us personally.

As combat pilots are briefed in the "ready room," so Christians are briefed by God through their daily reading of the Bible. It is true that "all scripture is inspired by God and profitable for teaching, for reproof, for correction, and for training in righteousness, that the man of God may be complete, equipped for every good work" (2 Timothy 3:16, 17).

This briefing for immediate tasks and problems is the most important time of the Christian's day. With it we are fortified for all contingencies; without it we walk as crippled men, stumbling over pebbles and boulders.

Who of us does not need wisdom? The deepest wisdom of the ages is found through communion with the God of time and eternity. Who does not need guidance? We have God's promises to guide us if we acknowledge him above everything else. In the frustrations of our times, who does not need assurance? And in the Scriptures we find assurance that rises above any contingency.

What about the practical problems involved in daily devotions? The answers will vary with each person, but the general principles would seem to be the same:

1. Decide on a regular time and let nothing interfere

with it. If you ever get "too busy" to spend this time in prayer and Bible study, then you are indeed too busy! To permit laziness or trivialities or the routine pressures of daily living to interfere is like performing plastic surgery on a harelip while the patient is dying of cancer. I find early in the morning the ideal time for devotions. Others may prefer late at night or some other time. Each person must decide on a suitable time in the light of his own circumstances.

2. Find a quiet place where you will not be interrupted, some part of the house not frequented by others during that particular time.

3. Get a comfortable chair and use it. There is no reason to inflict punishment on the body, and every reason to be at ease.

4. Have good light so you can see without straining your eyes.

5. Have a notebook and pencil at hand. Spirit-directed thoughts and impressions, if written down, can be the basis for helpful conversations and teaching.

6. Get a fine-point red pencil and use it to underline passages of Scripture that speak to your heart as you read them. As time goes on, your Bible will itself become a commentary, and those underlined verses will catch your eye and refresh your memory.

7. With that red pencil use a six-inch plastic ruler to underline verses with straight lines.

8. As you read the Bible, have an attitude of openness to the Lord: ask him to speak to your heart; offer him your obedient will; request understanding to see the wonderful teachings of the Holy Spirit. And as you read, remind yourself of God's faithfulness, love, and power.

9. Use a good concordance. As you become familiar with more and more passages of which you remember only a word or two, you can find them again with a concordance. If you are studying by subjects or topics, get a topical Bible.

The daily devotional time should begin with a confession of sins in which we hide nothing from the One who sees and knows all. Upon confession, we know we have forgiveness, and with forgiveness there is healing and preparation for anything God may have in store for that day. When we have complied with these things God requires, we find ourselves on solid "praying ground."

The devotional time can become a joyous experience, for by it we are nourished in the things of the Spirit and prepared for the rigors of living. Although we do not know the future, the God of the future will make us sufficient for any and every thing when we rely on him.

A TIME TO WORSHIP

Theodore Roosevelt stated, "You may worship God anywhere at any time, but the chances are that you will not do so unless you have first learned to worship him in some particular place at some particular time."

David said, "I was glad when they said unto me, Let us go into the house of the Lord" (Psalm 122:1).

Thomas Carlyle said, "No greater calamity can befall a nation than the loss of worship."

—KNIGHT'S ILLUSTRATIONS FOR TODAY

THE SHEEP AND THE WOLVES

by Ray C. Stedman

Minister, Peninsula Bible Church, Palo Alto, California

Many Christians suffer today from ecclesiastical schizophrenia. On the one hand they are urged by pastors to withdraw from worldly associations and activities, and on the other to proclaim the gospel to perishing people. It is impossible to do both!

The true solution lies in a return to the biblical concept of separation. Our Lord Jesus put it in a nutshell when he said to his disciples: "Behold, I send you forth as sheep in the midst of wolves." What a strange situation! A human shepherd tries to keep his sheep as far away from the wolves as possible. Here is a Shepherd, the Good Shepherd, who deliberately sends his sheep out into the midst of wolves. That is where he wants them to be! He sent them there! Are not the sheep in danger? Of course they are! What is the protection for the individual sheep? It is only as he realizes his constant danger and remains in touch with his Shepherd; then, and then only, is he safe. The inward strength the Shepherd gives is sufficient to overcome the outward threat of the wolves.

The Lord Jesus said to his own: "As the Father has sent me, even so send I you into the world." How was he sent? As a Lamb, a Lamb among wolves; and though the wolves did their worst, yet the Lamb was triumphant in the end. Did Jesus not pray specifically to the Father about the disciples: "I pray not that thou shouldest take them out of the world" (whether actually or practically) "but that thou shouldest keep them from the evil one"?

And what form of separation did he practice when he was here? Did not the "separated" and pious Pharisees say of him: "This man eateth with publicans and sinners"? They did not say this with malice; they said it with a gasp. They were amazed at his willingness to mix with sinners.

They were afraid he would be defiled by such contact. But he never was. Instead, he drew many from among the publicans and sinners to himself and cleansed away their defilement with his own purity.

"But," you say, "the Lord was God manifested in the flesh. I dare not mix with sinners as he did, for I have not his strength and purity." Yes, you have! What else does it mean: "Christ in you, the hope of glory"? "I can do all things through Christ who strengtheneth me." Does he not say: "As the Father hath sent me, even so send I you into the world"? Are not all his resources at our disposal?

Does the Lord, then, want his people to withdraw from all worldly associations and activities? Absolutely not! He wants us to mix with the world, eat with unbelievers, make friends with them, enter into their homes, and invite them freely into ours. But he wants us to remember that in so doing we are in great danger. We are sheep in the midst of wolves. One failure to maintain contact with the Shepherd, one little yielding to the wolves' enticement to be as they are, and the whole pack will converge, hopeful for a kill. It is a place of great danger. But it is the place where the Lord wants us to be. Christians are expected to live on a spiritual frontier, ever alert to the danger without, ever drawing upon the Strength within.

But what about John's warning, "Love not the world, neither the things that are in the world"; and James' sharp word, "Know ye not that the friendship of the world is enmity with God?" Exactly! They both warn about the same thing: the danger involved in being sheep amongst wolves. It is not friendship for the worldling that is dangerous but friendship for the *world* that the worldling loves. As long as the sheep acts as God's sheep, he is safe in the wolf's den; but when he forgets what he is and begins to think as a wolf, then he is in terrible danger. Thus Christians are to use the things of the world circumspectly but not to love them. To regard them as of great importance is enmity with God.

This understanding of separation is a far cry from any

boredom and frustration of a monastic nature. It is, instead, a thrilling and daring challenge, appealing to the God-given love of adventure in every person. The Christian life becomes colorful and engrossing because it is fraught with danger and offers the exhilaration of successful combat with dark and sinister forces.

Further, such a concept makes Bible study and prayer exceedingly vital and useful. There is nothing like an awareness of danger to make an individual interested in weapons and strategy and the nature of the enemy. For spiritual danger, where is such help found? Only in the pages of Scripture and the place of prayer.

Is it not obvious that a separation which seeks to remove all danger also removes much incentive to growth and accomplishment? Has not the attempt to raise children in a totally Christian environment — schools, friends, societies, parties, etc. — produced a generation of mollycoddles who lack both interest and ability to influence the non-Christian world for Christ?

If this is true, we the parents and pastors and Sunday school teachers are at fault for letting them grow up without teaching them how to fight the good fight of faith. We have conditioned them to avoid evil — not to overcome it; and when they finally must face an evil world, they easily succumb or try to run away. A few are able to make emergency adjustments and survive until they learn by necessity to become good soldiers of Christ.

We must listen again to the words of our Lord: "As the Father hath sent me, even so send I you — to do my work, that of reaching and winning the lost — in my way, by becoming their friend, their confidant, their companion — exposed to my dangers, the allurement of the world, the selfishness of the flesh, and the independence of the devil — but overcoming with my weapons: faith in God, knowledge of his Word, personal righteousness, perseverance in prayer, and loving not your lives unto death." This is his command; we must prepare ourselves and our children to obey!

But someone asks: "What shall we do with the words,

222 /

'Be ye not unequally yoked together with unbelievers'?" Admittedly, these words appear to sanction an isolationist type of separation. But they only appear to do so. Carefully considered, they lend strong support to the sheep-among-wolves concept we believe our Lord wants his own to follow.

Take the matter of the yoke, for example. This is a clear reference to Deuteronomy 22:10, where the people of God were warned: "Thou shalt not plow with an ox and an ass together." This was because of the differing natures of the two beasts, the ass customarily walking much faster than the ox, and reacting differently to various commands. It would be exceedingly frustrating to both beasts to be yoked together, and little could be accomplished. But nothing was said against an ass and an ox associating together or being placed in the same pasture, watering and feeding together, etc. It was the "yoke" that was forbidden, for it involved a union of forces which neither animal was free to break voluntarily.

So Christians may associate freely with unbelievers, even to joining clubs and associations where their mutual interests meet, as long as such association does not commit them legally or morally to some act or practice from which a mere word of dissent could not excuse them. Marriage is such a yoke, for it involves legal commitments beyond the mere will of the individual. Churches have rightly held that this passage forbids the marriage of Christian and non-Christians. A business partnership may likewise be such a yoke, though under most circumstances an employer-employee relationship cannot be considered so. There are borderline areas here where each person must be fully persuaded in his own mind about the proper action, and others need to remember that "to his own master a man standeth or falleth."

Christians could well remember the words of Thoreau: "If I do not seem to keep step with others, it is because I am listening to another drumbeat."

We must keep step with the "other drumbeat" at all costs. But we must remember that when our Commander walked in tune with it here in this world, it did not prevent him from eating and drinking with sinners, or from being known as "the friend of sinners." God has called us to be distinct, not to be distasteful. We are to be separated unto God, not separated from others. We must deliberately seek the place "where cross the crowded ways of life" and there sing: "In the cross of Christ I glory." That is the place of danger, but it is the place our Lord wants us to be — as sheep in the midst of wolves. Only when we are in that place shall we be able to fulfill our commission: "As the Father hath sent me, even so send I you."

Someone asked a businessman, "What's your occupation?"

"I'm a Christian," was his reply.

"No, no," said the man. "I mean what's your job?"

The reply was the same. "I'm a Christian."

"You don't understand. I mean what do you do for a living?"

"My full-time occupation is to be a Christian, but I am a meat packer to pay expenses."

—UNITED METHODIST

AMBASSADOR TO THE WORLD

by Richard C. Halverson

President, International Christian Leadership

Talk about infiltration! Communism cannot hold a candle to Christ's witnesses around the world. Christ has his men everywhere. The real impact of the Church is not a huge religious combine or power bloc, overpowering by sheer force of numbers. It is not a massive show of solidarity or institutional might. The power of Christ's Church is infinitely more subtle, infinitely more effective.

The divine strategy is the Christian man, at his job day-in, day-out, bearing witness to Christ by life and lip right where he lives and works and plays. In business and industry, government and the professions, labor, education, the military, in strategic places around the world — behind the Iron Curtain, probably right in the Kremlin and Peking (he had men in Caesar's household in Paul's day) — Christ has his witnesses.

The Christian labor leader, businessman, military officer, policeman, surgeon, dentist, architect, merchant, farmer, lawyer, in Congress and parliaments, in the Pentagon and the State Department, in banks and clubs and lodges, in coal mines and steel mills — by the tens of thousands, by the millions — working, living for Christ. This is the real picture of authentic Christian influence.

It isn't what happens on Sunday morning in the sanctuary that is the measure of the influence of the Church, but what happens when the sanctuary is deserted; what happens Monday through Saturday in your home, office, on your job, in your social set. You are the Church, and it is your influence that is counting for or against Christ.

Actually the mission of the Church begins right outside its doors. Wherever there is a man or woman or child unevangelized, there is the mission of the Church. Jesus mildly rebuked his disciples on one occasion with words which awakened them to this fact: "Say not there are yet four months and then cometh the harvest. Lift up your eyes unto the fields already white unto harvest." Just look around you; that's where the mission of the Church begins!

One of the common ailments of the American Christian is this paradoxical excitement over the salvation of a head-hunter in Formosa or a pygmy in Africa or an Indian in the hinterland of Brazil, meanwhile ignoring the neighbor next door who is just as lost without Jesus Christ. And incidently, this attitude gets its reaction on the part of the "natives." They find it difficult to understand why Americans feels so strongly the necessity of preaching exclusively to "foreigners" when there is much evidence of need right at home.

The acid test of one's genuine concern for the foreign mission of the Church is his concern for the friend next door. The whole mission of the Church is evangelism, the winning of the lost to Christ, and evangelism begins right where the Church is, right where the Christian is. One certainly will not be evangelistic in another location if he is not evangelistic where he is!

Every true Christian should have the world on his heart! That is, he should be willing to settle for nothing less than evangelism worldwide. Not that every Christian is to try to go everywhere doing everything for everybody, but as each person does his job where he is and prays for laborers to be sent wherever God directs, each Christian's mission field will be the world and each will be following Christ's call day-in and day-out where the Lord has placed him.

Often the question is asked, "Why do we preach to people of other nations who have their own religion? Is it not arrogant and presumptuous of us to try to get them to exchange their religion for ours?" This is a good question and it has an adequate answer.

In the first place, it is incorrect to think of the goal of the missionary as being an attempt to get a "native" to exchange his religion for ours. Rightly understood, Christianity is infinitely more than religion. The message of the Christian missionary is the message of eternal life through Jesus Christ. Religion is man's effort to find God or placate an angry God for his sins. Christianity is the *good news* that God has come in Christ to forgive man's sins and offer him the gift of eternal life.

Remember that the religionists of Jesus' day represented his strongest opposition. They were incorrigibly hostile to Jesus and did not rest until they had liquidated him. In the light of history, religion can mean almost anything. Religion can lead to the most inhuman practices, such as infanticide, child brides, the burial alive of the wife or servants of the deceased, the worship of animals or fire or water or anything man cannot understand or control. It makes man bow down before the most grotesque inventions of his own hands. It has led to human sacrifice and the worst kind of human degradation.

Some of the wars and the most terrible atrocities that have scandalized history were perpetrated in the name of religion. The deplorable conditions under which some men live are due to their religion, not in spite of it.

But the mission of the Christian Church, when it is rightly understood, is not a matter of trying to get people to scrap their religion for another. It is to get them to embrace the gospel of Jesus Christ which has the power to redeem human nature from the terrible pit into which it has fallen. It is to tell them of the love of God in Christ and to urge them to receive God's loving provision for their eternal welfare.

The core of Christianity is not the ethics and doctrines of Christ, but his death and resurrection. The message of the missionary has to do with events, not ideas. (See 1 Corinthians 15:1-4.)

Jesus Christ died that man might live. Apart from him there is no life, either on this earth or in the future. Only Jesus Christ holds out any hope for the sinner (no other religion has a redemptive force; no other religion is redemptive). Only in the gospel is "the power of God unto salvation for everyone that believes."

While speaking at the Pacific School of Religion to several hundred pastors, Emil Brunner was asked, "Do you really believe that Jesus Christ is the only way to God?" The noted theologian answered, "There is a verse of Scripture which says, 'There is no other name under heaven given among men whereby we must be saved.' Do you expect me to quarrel with that?"

Annually Christian churches spend millions of dollars on foreign missions enterprise. The practical question rises: Why is such a large amount invested in the foreign mission of the Church? What is the real justification for missions?

Is it the poverty of the people? This is important. No Christian can be aware of the desperate plight of the masses of Asia, for example, without having some compassion, some desire to help. But this is not the justification for missions.

Is it in order that we may share "our way of life" with the peoples of the world? Hardly, though we may feel our way is best. In many cases Western culture has been a destructive force uprooting people from their ancient cultures and not bringing faith in Christ.

Is it to alleviate man's misery? Worthy as this is, it falls short of the real objective of foreign missions.

There is one overwhelming reason for the foreign missions enterprise. The one dominating motive for the mission of the Church, the justification for the millions invested in it annually, is that Jesus Christ commanded his Church to do this!

The last thing he said before ascending to the Father (Acts 1:8) was to challenge his church to be witnesses of the gospel to the "uttermost parts of the earth." This was his mandate! The Church that does not promote foreign missions energetically is guilty of disobeying what the Lord commanded us to do. We must, if we are to call Jesus our Lord, be everlastingly at the job of telling everybody everywhere of the love of God in Christ. "Ye shall receive power, after that the Holy Spirit is come upon you; and ye shall be witnesses unto me both in Jerusalem, and in all Judea, and in Samaria, and unto the uttermost part of the earth" (Acts 1:8).

There are many ways of witnessing to the love of God as it has been given in Jesus Christ. It is hardly worthwhile to speak of God's love if one does not demonstrate that love in his life. Perhaps no single thing has alienated as many people from Christ as loveless Christians.

God's love is expressed in many ways on the mission field: in the work of healing by medical missions; in the work of charity by the welfare agencies of the Church; in the work of compassion in orphanages, widows' homes, schools for the blind and deaf and crippled; in the work of education and agriculture. But important as these are, they are not primary. Evangelism is the primary task of the mission enterprise. All these others support the primary work. The first great missionary, the Apostle Paul, went out with only one thing: a message. It was this message, ratified by the love and sacrifice of Christians, that turned the Roman Empire upside down in a generation.

Jesus left a mandate to his Church to go into the world, beginning at home, and preach the gospel. And he left his Church the power to carry out the mandate. He sent the Holy Spirit to be the power. He committed to his Church the ministry of reconciliation and he gave his Church the Holy Spirit to enable her to fulfill the ministry. The commission is binding on every Christian, and the Holy Spirit indwells every Christian.

The Holy Spirit is the power of the Christian witness, the Christian mission. Whether it is the missionary actively engaged in evangelism on the field, or the layman faithfully witnessing in his community or on his job, the power of the witness is the same — the Holy Spirit. "If you then, being evil, know how to give good gifts unto your children; how much more shall your heavenly Father give the Holy Spirit to them that ask him?" (Luke 11:13)